Honeymooners Forever

Honeymooners Forever

Twelve Step Marriage Survival Guide

Phoebe Hutchison

Rekindle Publishing
Melbourne Victoria Australia

HONEYMOONERS FOREVER
Phoebe Hutchison

Published by Rekindle Publishing
P.O. Box 842, Somerville, Victoria, 3912, Australia.

Disclaimer
The material contained in this book is not intended as medical advice. If you have a medical issue or illness, consult a qualified physician. The intent of the author is to offer information of a general nature to assist you in your relationship. In the event you use any of the information for yourself, which is your constitutional right, the author and publisher assume no responsibility for your actions.

National Library of Australia
Cataloguing-in-Publication Entry

Hutchison, Phoebe (Phoebe Louise).
Honeymooners forever : twelve step marriage survival guide.

1st ed.
Bibliography.
ISBN 9780646472331 (pbk.).

1. Marriage. 2. Married people – Life skills guides. 3. Interpersonal relations. 4. Parent and child. 5. Married people – Finance, Personal. I. Brown, Michelle (Michelle Louise). II. Winters, Wendy (Wendy Valmai). III. Tatham, Ryan (Ryan Lucas). IV. Title. (Series : Honeymooners forever).

306.81

Editors: Michelle Brown and Wendy Winters
Illustrations: Ryan Tatham
Typesetting by Midland Typesetters, Australia

For further information about this book visit the author's web site:
http://www.honeymoonersforever.com.au

May
the words
in this book
bring you joy
touch your souls
and transform your marriage
in a most magnificent way
from this day forth.

The Twelve Steps

1. Treat your partner like a lover — not a spouse
2. Be yourself and allow your partner to be himself
3. Communicate well every day
4. Invest time and money in your relationship weekly
5. Stop finding fault and start praising
6. Plan the romance
7. Restore the passion
8. How to avoid or survive an affair
9. Children should enhance, not destroy, your marriage
10. Argue effectively
11. Improve your financial situation
12. Avoid or survive everything else life throws at you

Marriage is the biggest roller-coaster ride of your life.
These steps will make the ride easier and more enjoyable.

Contents

The Twelve Steps   vi
Acknowledgments   xv
Foreword   xvii
Introduction   xix

Step One
Treat your partner like a lover — not a spouse   1
   Treat him like a prince   2
   Why should I be the one who changes?   2
   Listen to your partner   3
   Take an interest in your partner   3
   Notice the way you treat your partner   4
   Do you treat him poorly?   5
   Do you treat the children better than him? 5
   Do you treat your partner like a child?   6
   Men show their love differently   7
   Observe the way he treats his mother   7
   Falling in love   8
   Falling out of love   8
   The two types of romantic love   9
   Staying in love   10
   Are you an infatuation junkie?   10
   Case Study: Patricia   10
   Homework: Study other couples   12

Step Two

Be yourself and allow your partner to be himself	13
Please yourself	14
Do what you love doing to feel truly alive	14
Fulfil your dreams and have no regrets	15
Your friends are important	16
Your partner is only the icing on the cake	16
Your work affects your marriage	17
Keep your life in balance	18
Some time apart is great	18
Too much time apart can be harmful	19
Have your own hobbies	19
Don't be a prisoner in your marriage	20
Accept your partner	21
Women and work	22
Men and work	22
Don't be a marriage martyr	23
Case Study: Meaghan	23
Homework: If you love him, but you're not *in love* with him	25
What are you *not* doing with your life?	26

Step Three

Communicate well every day	27
Have daily chats	28
Do you find your man needs 'unwind time'?	28
Be your partner's best friend	28
Breakfast, Dinner and Bed Time	29
Know what you want	30
Don't settle for an average marriage	30
Be honest with yourself	31
Be honest with your partner	31

Do fun things together 32

Laugh together 32

Ask for what you want and need 33

Case study: Roger 34

Letter to my wife 34

Letter to my husband 35

Homework: Keep communication flowing.
Don't hold back 36

Step Four

Invest time and money in your relationship weekly 37

Invest time in grooming 38

Invest money in your relationship 38

Have a weekly family afternoon 39

Make your partner a priority 39

Case Study: Leanne 39

Anthony 40

Homework: Have a weekly date night 41

Step Five

Stop finding fault and start praising 43

Praise your partner daily 44

Try not to criticize your partner 45

Nitpickers Beware! 45

Stop complaining and start outsourcing 46

Avoid bitching sessions 46

The grass is not always greener 47

My story — over a decade ago 48

My story — now 49

Homework: Never complain about your partner
to other people 50

Step Six
Plan the Romance   51
  Look ready for romance   53
  Clothes make the man   53
  Dress sexy and you'll feel sexy   54
  Does hubby prefer the natural look?   54
  Flirt with your partner daily   55
  Is your bedroom like a hotel room?   55
  Interview with a 'spy for women'   56
  Homework: Do up your bedroom together   59

Step Seven
Restore the passion   61

Part A: Problems in the bedroom
  Part A: Problems in the bedroom   63
  Married women and sex   64
  Married men and sex   64
  Differing sexual appetites   65
  Men and women are different   66
  Are you a habitual leg crosser?   66
  8 Reasons why you may be rejecting him   67
  Sexual frustration in men   70
  Sexual frustration in women   71
  Don't just lie there   71
  Men need to chase   72
  Homework: Wives who neglect their husbands 73

Part B: Ideas & Suggestions
  Part B: Ideas & Suggestions   75
  Praise — Make your man feel like a stud   76
  Show him what you want   76
  Foreplay makes *all* the difference   77
  Not in the mood? Try a little O.F.F.   77
  Standard Foreplay vs Advanced Foreplay   78

Having sex is like eating a nice meal	78
Sex is all about give and take	79
There is more to life than missionary	79
Four basic types of sex	80
The female orgasm	81
The three main types of female orgasms	82
Not having orgasms?	83
The Big O — ten tips for more orgasms	84
Create a mood	85
Dirty Talk	85
Sexy clothing — Lingerie — Kinky Toys	86
Clothing, Lingerie, Toys & Accessories	86
Fantasies and Games	87
Dress-ups for two	87
Striptease	88
Dirty dancing at home	88
Sex Show for one	89
A man with erection has altered perception	90
Let your nightie say it all	90
Middle of the night romps	91
Star in your own video	92
Buy some mirrors for the bedroom	92
Interview: Sex worker	92
Homework: It's all in the eyes	100
Hot night workout	100
Quiz: How well do you know each other?	101

Step Eight

How to avoid or survive an affair	103
Keep sexual thoughts on your partner	104
The Mind Equation	104

The Mind Equation relating to fantasies 105
5 reasons why people have an affair 106
Your mind can lead you into an affair 108
Flirting: The two different types 109
Be careful who you flirt with 110
Internet affairs 110
After baby affair 111
Scent based sexual attraction 112
Are you too busy working? 114
You don't need a spare partner 114
Affairs destroy the soul 114
Stopping an affair 115
What if your partner is having an affair? 115
There are two sides to every affair 116
Avoid affairs by keeping your distance 116
Emotional affairs (triangles) 117
My emotional affair 118
Do you actually love the other person? 119
Case Study: Inside the mind of a mistress 120
Interview: Bull (player) 121
Quiz: Are you having an emotional affair? 127
Quiz: Are you heading for an affair? 128
Quiz: Is your partner having an affair? 129

Step Nine

Children should enhance, not destroy, your marriage 131
Childbirth changes a woman forever 132
Childbirth is like a little hurricane 132
Creating balance in your life 132
Teach your children about life 133
Praise your children daily 133
Never argue in front of children 134
Circle of life 135
Homework: Have a weekly children's night 137

Step Ten

Argue effectively   139
Don't be scared to argue   140
Three 'Golden Argument rules'   140
When did the fighting begin?   142
Resentment destroys marriages   142
Ten quick tips for resolving conflict   143
My favourite tip: keep yourself happy   147
Don't sweep your problems under a rug   148
Don't let your house become a war zone   148
Messy home, messy mind, messy life   148
Case Study: Terrie   149
Homework: Do a R & P Check list (Quiz)   150

Step Eleven

Improve your financial situation   151
Free yourself of debt   152
Save then buy   152
Money is not the root of all evil   153
Bills are a part of life   153
Teach your children about money   154
Money is made in the mind first   155
Case Study: Ben and Lisa   155
Homework: Start saving 10% of all you earn   156

Step Twelve

Avoid or survive everything else life throws at you   157
Avoid living in the wrong house   158
Avoid clingy friends   159
Survive angry outbursts and tantrums   160
Avoid violence in your marriage   161
Interview with a survivor of violence   162
Survive the wedding   165

Survive the first year of marriage   166
Survive a midlife crisis   167
Survive workaholics   168
Survive working together   169
Survive PMT   169
Survive depression   170
Quiz: Depression (the mindset)   171
Quiz: Depression (get your life back)   172
Survive jealousy in the marriage   173
Survive the mother-in-law   174
Survive gaining weight   175
Survive your nightmares and dreams   176
Survive marrying a clone of your parent   177
Survive a break up   178
Survive finding the perfect man   179
Survive family   180
Case Study: Bianca   180
Homework: Don't give up on love, just because
   you think it is easier   182

About the Author   183
Recommended Reading   187

Acknowledgments

I would like to thank the many women and men who have spoken to me over the past few years about their marriages. You opened your hearts and gave me an honest glimpse into your marriages and lives. Often it was your success, or pain, which inspired me to work harder and finish this book. Funnily enough, it seemed like every time I put my pen, or laptop, down and thought about something else, another marriage in crisis presented itself. Your shared pain will help other couples have more fulfilling marriages.

To protect the confidentiality of all the people I have spoken to about their marriages, I have changed the names used throughout this book.

I would like to thank my family and friends for their never ending support and love.

I would like to thank my best friend, Simone, for being an integral part of the research. During many fun-filled lunches, or over coffee or drinks, we bounced ideas and theories around, making the creation of this book possible.

Thank you to my cartoonist, Ryan Tatham, for being a creative genius and creating exactly what I wanted.

I would like to express my deepest gratitude to Wendy Winters, who was like my second brain, for all her editing hours.

I would like to thank my grammar and copy editor, Michelle

Brown, for her attention to detail, advice, much needed assistance and professionalism.

Finally, I would like to thank my husband for always supporting me in the pursuit of my dreams and for being trustworthy, handsome, funny, intelligent, sexy, romantic, a great father to our children, hard working, my best friend and my soul mate.

Foreword

'When God joined man and woman together he must have been joking!' Many married couples have expressed these sentiments. And when you think about it, it is a strange combination. But when a relationship between a man and a woman is working well, what an unbeatable combination. Have you ever thought how simple life would be if women married other women? Now let's be serious, a man is nowhere near as *bitchy* as a woman can be. Can you imagine two women living together, forever? They would get PMT together and end up killing each other. Imagine the jealousy, the rivalry and the nasty comments. Not to mention the fights over the mirror. The nagging would continue all day and night.

Mere men, however, seem to be unchanging. We women change with our clothes, our hormones, the moon, and our cravings. Men hardly change. Day in, day out: same man. (There are some exceptions of course). God put thought into this little equation: Stable man with ever-changing woman.

Marriage involves two people from different backgrounds, gene pools, childhoods and attitudes. In addition, each day your lives are constantly changing. Yet you're supposed to be as one, mind, body and soul, forever more. The bodies' becoming one is not usually the hard part; it's the minds and souls that need to stay connected for this union to remain intact.

Marriage comes with one guarantee: marriage is not always easy. Don't feel like a failure if you are struggling with your marriage. All happily married couples find marriage a struggle at different times.

Introduction

Every marriage has the potential to be awesome. If your marriage has become boring or a daily struggle, or if you are considering separation or divorce, then I have some good news: I have spent the last ten years finding the secrets of happily married couples. By documenting, testing and sharing these secrets with married couples, all the ground work has been done. Now you can simply start using the steps, and transform your marriage, with the flick of a few pages.

This book was written with unhappily married couples in mind; not just to save them, but to totally transform them. Why live in a marriage that is not awesome, romantic and wonderful?

These steps will help you have the marriage of your dreams. How do I know? Well, I have been in the marriage of my dreams since I began using the steps a decade ago. Yet before then, I felt like I was living in a shell of a previously happy marriage. I felt totally empty. I was a resentful and unhappy wife. I would get knots in my stomach just being in the same room as my husband. Now, ten years later, I am with the same husband, yet I totally adore him.

These steps work — but not like a recipe for a cake. You cannot simply use the steps, and then store them in the top of your pantry to look at in another year. For the best results, keep a copy of the steps on your fridge or in your wallet. Then you can refer to them often, especially if you start arguing or feeling distant from your spouse.

This book is different because I am not a doctor, psychologist or counsellor. I am a married, working, mother of two. I can relate to working mothers because I am writing from the trenches. Everything I am writing about has either worked for me, or for other women I have spoken to.

Why am I so passionate about saving marriages? Well, I love being married and I love the institution of marriage. Having a partner for life, who supports you in your dreams and grows old with you, is simply beautiful. Waking up next to the person you adore, is such a gift. It's wonderful to know that at any moment you can put your arms around someone who loves you deeply. Your husband knows you better than any one else, and is your best friend, who shares every detail of your life with you. You married your husband, your soul mate, so that when you need a soft place to fall, he is there.

A marriage should never be thrown away. Marriage, like a diamond, can be picked up, polished, and sparkle again with the brilliance of the sun.

Step One

Treat your partner like a lover — not a spouse

You cannot change someone else. You can only change yourself. If you change, then your partner will change. Create this miracle in your marriage today.

Treat him like a prince

Before you can improve the way you treat your partner, you need to be consciously aware of the way you act towards him. Ask yourself the following questions:

- Do I kiss and cuddle my partner when he comes home or goes out?
- Do we hold hands while we are out together?
- Do my eyes light up when my partner enters the room?
- Do I make him feel loved and adored every day?
- Do I make a habit of flirting with my partner?
- Am I treating my partner poorly? If so, how often?

If you want to be treated like a princess, treat him like a prince. So run up to your prince and start kissing him enthusiastically, while giving him a big hug, whenever he walks through the door. Surely you want to feel that you're spending your life with your lover and best friend? Then it makes sense to treat them that way.

One woman recently told me that her partner had a disorder. She said, 'He wants to be worshipped!' After I stopped laughing, I simply told her that *all* men have this disorder. All men have an inbuilt need to be worshipped, if not by their partners, then by someone else. Treat your partner like a lover, not a spouse. It is the quickest way I know to turn an unhappy marriage around.

Why should *I* be the one who changes?

Women often ask this question when I suggest they start treating their partners better. The answer is this: people are born copycats. In addition, because the bond between a husband and wife is so strong, if you change, your partner can't help but change. For example, when you join a gym or start dieting, ever notice how all of a sudden hubby starts cutting down on the beer and biscuits? Or when you plan a makeover for the garden, isn't he the one driving you down to the hardware store? So, why is your treatment of each other any different? It's simply not. You change, and he will.

Most married couples, like it or not, are mere reflections of each other. In many ways, you are not two, but one unit, going through life together. Therefore, when you change, you are changing the energy in your part of the unit, which in turn affects the entire unit. Any changes you make dramatically affect the core of the marriage, whether they are good or bad changes.

Listen to your partner

We need to spend time talking about our lives, children and work, every day. Let your partner enjoy turning to you. Try to have at least one talking and listening session each day and listen to your partner whenever he talks. If you're not interested in what he is talking about, then become interested. If you cannot listen at that moment, tell him. And make a time to listen later that day. Never pretend to listen.

One of the easiest ways to make someone feel special and loved is to listen to them. Listening is an essential ingredient in all great friendships.

Take an interest in your partner

Almost everybody has one thing in their life with which they are totally obsessed. Naturally, we want our partner to take an interest in these passions of ours. Yet, many people find their partner shows no interest in what really matters to them. This can lead to a person feeling neglected and emotionally disconnected, which causes problems in the relationship.

Ten years ago I paid absolutely no attention to my partner's longwinded rambling about computers. I was too focused on my own life goals. Thank goodness my attitude changed. Now I not only listen to him, but I work for him in his internet business. I share a passion for his passion, and I have a part-time job which I love.

When you take an interest in your partner's passions, it adds great value and a new dimension to your relationship. Sadly, one of the reasons people have affairs is because someone else listens and pays attention to them. Now that's another important reason to start listening to your partner and showering him with attention.

Notice the way you treat your partner

Have you noticed the way you treat someone, is often the way they behave? Your attitude towards your partner has a dramatic impact on how he will act. If you treat him like an irresponsible, lazy loser, he will most probably act that way. If you show him endless love, respect, and trust, he is more likely to act lovable, trustworthy, and respectable. Phillip C McGraw talks about a similar concept — 'We teach people how to treat us'— in his life-changing book, *Life Strategies*. The way you treat your partner every single day makes a huge difference to how great your marriage remains.

Do you treat him poorly?

In most cases, his treatment of you mirrors your treatment of him. If your partner is treating you poorly, ask yourself, 'Am I treating him the way I would like to be treated?' Would *you* enjoy being married to you? Do you treat your partner badly? Do you swear at him, belittle him, neglect him, yell at him, not listen to him, reject him sexually, take him for granted, nag him, boss him around, criticize or try to control him? Why would he bring you flowers, stare into your eyes with wonder and smother you with kisses and cuddles, if you are treating him this way?

It is simple. You get what you give. Of course, there are exceptions to this rule:

a. Some men treat their wives terribly, irrespective of how their wives treat them.
b. Some men will worship their bitchy, nasty partners, to the complete surprise of all those around them.

The good news is it's possible to change a bad habit into a good one, in as little as ten days. You just need to be consistent in repeating your new habits until you find yourself saying, 'Hello darling. How was your day at work?' while running up and kissing him on the lips, without even realizing you're doing it.

Do you treat the children better than him?

Mother Nature ensures mothers devote huge amounts of time and energy to their children. This is obviously for the sake of every child's emotional and physical well-being, but some mothers find it difficult to switch some of their love and attention back to their husbands. They end up giving so much to their children they simply have nothing left to give their partners at the end of each day. They spend hours fussing over their children, going to all their children's extra curricular activities, talking endlessly about their children's achievements, while neglecting their own husbands.

Don't both partners decide to have children together as a team? It wouldn't be possible without the man. Yet many husbands are pushed aside, neglected, physically and emotionally, and made to feel like sperm donors. All because their wives fall in love with their children and out of love with their husbands.

In some cases, fathers treat their children better than they treat their wives. In one marriage I knew of, the husband would come home and not even kiss his wife hello. Instead, he would rush off and play with the children. Sure he looked like a 'super dad', but his wife was always jealous and resentful due to this unequal attention. Sadly this marriage did not last.

If either you or your partner is putting the children first, then this habit can change. As long as you are aware of the problem you can do something about it. Husband neglect is an issue in many marriages experiencing problems. How alienating for a man when his wife practically ignores him after they have children.

Do you treat your partner like a child?

In a healthy give and take relationship, partners naturally turn to one another for advice. Yet over time, it's easy to forget that hubby once did things by himself, and made up his own mind, without our opinion all the time. However, some women go even further than offering advice. They treat their partners like children by becoming really controlling, interfering, or bossy.

Being bossed around, dominated, or treated like a child by their wife is humiliating for a man. So, next time you feel a criticism bubbling up — swallow it! At least think it through before you say it. Will your insults and put downs help your relationship? Or are you simply just letting off steam? Criticizing your partner is an extremely harmful habit to adopt, and never productive. He may turn into someone you can't respect anymore, as no one respects a doormat. He may become bitter, emotionally withdrawn, or even leave you for a less critical partner.

If you want your man to be a strong, independent hero-type, who will look after you throughout life's storms, don't treat him like a child. Treat him like your own personal hero. He deserves to be treated with the same care and consideration as when you first started dating.

Men show their love differently

You may look at your partner and wonder if they really love you enough, as they don't tell you ten times a day. You may show them how you feel by cuddling them, and telling them you love them, constantly. Yet they may not be running up to you and hugging you as much as you would like. Well, this is because a man will show his love for his wife by doing things for her, and for the family, like mowing the lawn, fixing the broken fence, or putting oil in her car.

So next time you think he doesn't love you enough, think of all the wonderful things he has done for you, and for the family, during the past week.

Observe the way he treats his mother

If your boyfriend or fiancé treats his mother badly — beware. Often the way a man treats his mother, is a clear indication of how he will treat his future wife. Sigmund Freud suggests in the Oedipus complex that the relationship a man has with his mother profoundly affects every other relationship he has with a woman.

So next time you meet his mother, watch closely. Hopefully he's kind and caring towards her, and not nasty.

Falling in love

When you first fall in love, your new partner is all you can think about. The blood rushing though your veins is full of endorphins due to the infatuation. These endorphins are commonly called 'happy hormones' as they make people feel happy, vibrant and alive. While infatuated, you often have trouble eating and sleeping and have extra energy and a huge passion for life. Love songs sound as if they are written for you and your partner, and if you are not with your partner, you are most likely daydreaming about him.

It may all sound like a teenager's diary, but when the love-bug bites it doesn't matter how old you are, you fall in love the same way. Some people feel infatuated for three months, others for eighteen months, but twelve months is the typical length of an infatuation. Infatuation is the glue that keeps people together through the early stages of a relationship.

Falling out of love

However, as time goes by and the infatuation wears off, the complexities of life, i.e. work, getting married, having children, paying bills, place strain on the relationship. When the infatuation wears off you will see your partner in a more honest light, warts and all, like a true picture in front of you. Ideally you should not love him less — just differently. This is the delicate time in a relationship when many couples break-up, or many marriages fail. During this time many couples no longer blinded by infatuation may discover they are not actually compatible with their partners. When the infatuation fades, you start to feel a more 'comfortable love' rather than a 'passionate love'. Your partner feels more like a brother than a lover. And as you become aware of their bad points, disagreements and arguments start to occur more often. Some people panic when they don't feel the same magic as before. Many couples become less active in the bedroom due to hormonal changes (less endorphins).

There is an old joke about this drop in sexual activity: If you put a jelly bean in a jar every time you have sex during the first year of marriage, and then take a jelly bean out of the jar every time you have sex after the first year of marriage — you'll never empty the jar. Don't panic yet. In a happy and passionate marriage, you will most certainly empty the jar.

The two types of romantic love

There are really two types of love: Infatuation (new) and real (lasting) love. Infatuation is the initial stage in the relationship. This type of love is all about goose bumps, obsession with your partner, being highly attracted to each other and seeing your partner as flawless. It's almost like living in 'fairyland' as you are often completely oblivious to their faults.

Real love is the lasting stage of the relationship. It begins after the infatuation passes. This type of love is all about deep friendship, commitment, loyalty, familiarity, sharing a home, having children and the ability to see and accept each other's differences.

Staying in love

You can keep the 'honeymoon feeling' alive forever, but this doesn't happen by accident. You need to work at it. While being infatuated (new love) and being in real love (lasting love) are two separate feelings, you can still feel like honeymooners forever. You can still lust after each other, be excited to spend time together, see mostly the good in each other and feel like you are dating forever.

Are you an infatuation junkie?

Some people find themselves jumping from relationship to relationship without realizing they have became addicted to the endorphins released during infatuation. To an outsider they may appear to be sleeping around, but in reality they are in love with the feeling of being in love. These people usually end relationships after about twelve months or so, when endorphins start to decrease. Do you know any friends or family who are like this?

* * *

Patricia was beautiful, vivacious and fun loving. At the time I met her, she was married to her third husband. As we chatted she revealed that she loved her husband, he was a wonderful man, but the passion had died and she was no longer sexually attracted to him. She lived in a beautiful home and her husband seemed like a caring and devoted man. He looked as though he adored her, but she felt no spark. She could not understand how I could possibly still feel passion and enthusiasm, after so many years, with the same man. The last time we spoke she said she was 'madly in love' with a work colleague. I did not find out what happened, but I can only assume she was heading towards her fourth marriage.

Patricia experiences the spice, the infatuation, and when it dies she looks elsewhere, because she thinks the relationship has become boring. She needs constant excitement, but has not discovered the joy of keeping the passion alive with the same person. In retrospect she appears to be an infatuation junkie.

Infatuation junkies may think there is something wrong with them. But perhaps they don't know about the two very different types of romantic love: infatuation (new love) and real love (lasting love)?

Homework

Study other couples

If it has been a long time since you started dating, and you need inspiration, watch couples who have just started dating. You may also want to study happily married couples.

Study and learn from them.

Watch the wonderful and loving way they treat each other.

Notice the way that they look at each other, talk to each other, and shower each other with attention and affection.

It does wonders to treat him like a lover, every single day. It quickly re-energizes any struggling relationship.

Remember to make this your new lifelong habit and watch your marriage troubles fade.

Step Two

Be yourself and allow your partner to be himself

Try not to change just because you are married. Let the unique qualities that first attracted you both to each other, be the glue that keeps you together forever.

Please yourself

While marriage is a huge adjustment, and both of you will change over time, it is vitally important to stay true to yourself and your needs. It is so sad when after marrying, one partner all of a sudden 'drops out of life' and lives for their spouse only. They end up doing what their partner wants to do all the time, and putting their own wants and needs aside.

Think back to when you were single and recall what you did for fun. Think about the plans you had for your life back then. Try not to fall into the habit of only considering what your partner wants. It's your life, after all.

Sometimes it is difficult to know what you want. My mother once asked me, 'If you had six months to live, what would you do?' Without hesitation, I replied, 'I would go on a cruise to Tasmania.' I had wanted to take that cruise my entire life but hadn't, as I was afraid of being seasick. So one weekend, my Mother and I bravely faced our fears and travelled to Tasmania by ship. The holiday was, without a doubt, one of the most memorable and enjoyable holidays I've ever had. Standing on the back of the ship, cruising across the ocean, I felt truly alive.

A happy person is somebody who is living their life the way they want to. Keep yourself happy, and allow your partner the freedom to do what makes them happy.

Do what you love doing to feel truly alive

When I was a professional singer, I would feel this unbelievable 'high' after a great performance. I was so exhilarated; it was as if I was walking on a cloud. I was sure I would never feel like that in any other job for the rest of my life. However, after a great day spent talking with clients, attending meetings or a seminar, I feel those feelings of elation again.

When we do what we love doing, we feel energized and vibrant. It's as if we are connected to the universal energy source. The energy flowing through our veins makes us feel fantastic. This is the buzz you get when you're doing what you want to do in life. You can also feel this buzz when you're doing what you're meant to be doing with your life.

Fulfil your dreams and have no regrets

Even more important than money is the feeling that you are doing what you are meant to be doing with your life — that you are on the right path. You need to pursue your dreams, goals and ambitions in your career and spare time. When you are fulfilled in your life, you bring a happier person to the relationship. You may want to use your talents to make a difference in this world, or to do something bizarre as a career, which your family doesn't approve of.

I have passionately chased every dream I have ever had, so has my partner. Even though I didn't get the record deal I chased for five years, I feel content knowing that I had given 100% to pursuing my dream. I don't want a record deal now, as I have a wonderful life, filled with family and my career which I love. I have no regrets.

My partner doesn't hold me back, just as I don't hold him back. We support each other. In all great marriages, both partners support each other through life, particularly when it comes to their ambitions and interests. You don't want to grow old and look back at your life with regret. Follow your passions and support your partner when he follows his passions.

Your friends are important

Naturally your partner should always feel loved and on the very top of your list of special people. However, that doesn't mean you can't see your friends anymore. You need friends, as your partner cannot possibly be the only person you talk to day in, day out. Having friends enables you to have a range of emotional needs fulfilled. Most people feel more content, and psychologically balanced, when they socialize regularly with their friends or family. When you get together with your partner, after spending time talking and laughing with friends, you will be a happier person.

Don't neglect the other people in your life. Just be careful you don't spend more time with them, than your partner. Your partner is the most valuable friend you will ever have.

Your partner is only the icing on the cake

When I was nineteen years old, I was temporarily unemployed, unhappy, and I didn't socialize. Every night I would expect my husband (my boyfriend at the time) to come over to my house and be my entertainment. I expected him to make me feel complete, satisfied and happy. Yet, it is *not* possible for another person to give you what you need to give to yourself: happiness and satisfaction in life.

Don't expect your partner to magically transform you from an unfulfilled person into a fulfilled and happy person. Your partner is the icing on the cake of your life, not the cake.

Your work affects your marriage

Whether you are working as a full-time mum, or working outside the home, it is important to enjoy what you are doing. Your work has a dramatic impact on your life and your marriage. It is vital that it leaves you feeling satisfied at the end of the day, at the very least. If you are lucky enough to love your work, that is even better.

We have a limited amount of hours per lifetime. Why spend hundreds of hours doing work that you don't like? Every day when you go to bed, you want to feel happy about getting up in the morning.

And as your life changes over time, you will need to re-evaluate your work preferences. Unsure of what you want to do? Make a list of everything you like doing, your good points and your skills. You may want to ask your friends and family to help. Armed with this list of your skills, you should be able to review your work choices.

Sadly many people continue to work in jobs that no longer suit them. And a great job to one person may be a nightmare to another. For example, while I found being a covers singer glamorous, after 450 gigs, over five years, I became tired of working every weekend. The weekdays were filled contacting agents and learning songs, and the weekends were spent getting ready for gigs and performing. I would not be happy today if I were a singer still working weekends. I prefer to spend my weekends with my family nowadays.

Throughout your life as you change, so do your ambitions. What you want to do today may be completely different from what you want to do in five years time. You may assume that because your partner studied at university to become a teacher, he will spend his whole life teaching. What if he teaches for a year and decides he doesn't like teaching anymore? A job you once loved could become a job you can't stand. It's common for people to start a career, and then decide to do something completely different later in life.

You cannot be happy in your life and have a great marriage, if you stay in an occupation that no longer suits you.

Keep your life in balance

For maximum peace and happiness you need to maintain the balance between work and play, especially when children are involved. Women in particular, need to maintain an even balance of work, socializing, relaxing, time alone, housework, paperwork, exercise, entertaining, husband time, children time and family time. If enough time is not allocated to any particular area, you are likely to become stressed. It is really important to know your limitations. If you keep your life balanced you will be a happier person and a better partner.

Some time apart is great

From time to time, do you find yourself getting a little 'clingy' with your spouse? Do you constantly ask him, 'what are we doing now' or 'have you got a minute'? Be careful not to suffocate your partner. If you spend too much time together, you may end up getting sick of each other. Have you ever noticed that when your partner goes away for a couple of days, you easily re-establish some of your much needed independence? You begin to feel more in tune with your wants and needs again. By doing things apart your relationship should remain 'fresh'. You should feel more excitement, intimacy, independence and romance in the relationship.

No matter how much you love each other, it is not natural to be 'glued to your partner', every minute of every day and night.

Too much time apart can be harmful

Although some time apart can be very beneficial to your relationship, it's not natural to live apart for most of the time. It simply doesn't work. Eventually you may become like strangers, as the emotional and spiritual connection is frequently severed. Switching constantly from 'single way of thinking' to 'married way of thinking' is difficult and confusing. I have seen and experienced the negative side of a partner working away from home too often. Spasmodic loneliness, managing the children alone and spending less time communicating, are all added pressures.

As a relationship grows, blossoms and evolves every single day, it's ideal to spend time with your partner each day. You married so that the two of you could be together, not apart.

Have your own hobbies

If you have your own interests and hobbies you will rarely feel bored. Fill your spare time with socializing, reading books or magazines, watching TV or DVDs, enjoying your children, or whatever else you love to do. Hobbies or sports add enjoyment to your life. A happy person is much more fun to be married to, than an unhappy person.

Don't be a prisoner in your marriage

Many spouses are holding their partners captive in their marriages, by controlling them. I call this the 'controlling spouse syndrome', and I witness it all the time. A controlling spouse will often expect their partners to stay home, not socialize and not pursue their hobbies or ambitions. These controlling spouses are often over protective, jealous, manipulative and sometimes violent. The marriage suffers because of one partner's over-bearing need to control the other. The controlled partner, unhappy due to having no freedom, being suffocated and oppressed, will often end up rebelling.

If you are a prisoner in your marriage, reclaim your life, even if it takes time. Start with small issues, and build up to larger ones, until you feel you have re-established your independence.

A lot of men are controlling by nature, so many women need to work at maintaining their independence. Many men just seem to want to sweep their wives away and lock them up like Rapunzel so that when they get home, dinner's on the table, the house is clean, the children are happy and they can unwind after a hard day at work.

I know I need to work constantly at keeping my independence. I have the most perfect 'controlling spouse example' of my own: My best friend rang me recently and asked if I could meet her for dinner that night. I said, 'fine,' and quickly prepared dinner for my family. I told my husband I was going out for dinner with my best friend and would be back in an hour or two. Well, he replied with, 'What! Are you mad? How could you go out for dinner at "family dinner time"? That's crazy!'.

He was extremely angry. I had to stop and think. If I cancelled this dinner with my friend, then I would be allowing him to control and manipulate me. After fifteen seconds or so of consideration, I replied, 'Love you, back later,' and said goodbye to the children. I rang him a few minutes later and he was fine. I could have said, 'Sorry, how silly of me to think of having a meal with my friend. I will cancel my plans, darling.' However, I will not be a prisoner in my marriage, so I went.

Every day we all have choices. We can choose to be controlled, or free.

I see examples of the 'controlling spouse syndrome' all the time. Some partners control their spouse by not sharing money. Keeping a partner on a tight purse string is a cruel, and common, type of control. Play money should be factored into the budget and distributed evenly to each partner, so he can buy a few beers and she can buy that pair of jeans, without all the guilt.

You signed marriage papers — not ownership papers. You don't want to feel restricted in your life just because you're married. Your partner doesn't own you.

Accept your partner

Are you trying to change your partner? Surely, when you started dating, you and your partner would have been happy with each other? Yet, over time, you may start wishing that your partner was different and try to change him. This happens frequently.

When you get married, you marry a whole package. You need to be yourself and you need your spouse to accept you as you are; to accept your choices, your dreams, your personality, your needs, your body, your clothing and music tastes. By the same token, you need to accept your partner as he is, whether he's a crazy flirt, messy, unreliable, lazy, hopeless with money, a workaholic or stubborn. Your wedding vows most likely said, 'I want to be your partner, forever . . . 'til death do us part'. They most certainly did not say. 'I want to make major modifications once the honeymoon's over.'

Celebrate and respect the differences between you and your partner, as these differences are part of the magic that will keep you together, forever.

Women and work

Women who have children have another focus, another area for great job satisfaction. Many happy mothers only need to work part-time to feel satisfied. Most women with children feel so fulfilled in their primary roles, as mothers and housewives, that paid work simply provides a nice social break from the house and the children.

Men and work

Work plays a huge role in the happiness of most men, more so than women. As most men work longer hours in their paid jobs than women, if they are unhappy in their work, it affects their lives dramatically. Men will often get depressed if they are unhappy in their work or if they are unemployed.

Similarly, a man's view of his status in society and his success is linked to his employment. In most cases, men also feel pressure being the breadwinner for the family. They are also extremely competitive with each other when it comes to income. Most women don't feel this sense of income competition. We are more focused on competing with regards to weight, clothing and our children's achievements. (And you thought men were simple creatures?)

Ask your partner if he is really enjoying his work. It's sad to say, but many men are so concerned about whether there is enough money to pay the bills, that they forget to consider whether they are still happy in their current line of work.

Don't be a marriage martyr

Some women don't pursue their passions because they put their partner's and children's needs before their own. They may give up a career they love, to stay at home and mind the children, or they may give up hobbies, interests and spending time with their friends. Over time, they transform from the person they were at the start of the relationship, to an unfulfilled and bitter person. They no longer have the same spark they had previously. Their relationship suffers, as resentment toward their partner builds. (Resentment is a major passion killer, so naturally they suffer from a reduced sex drive). These marriage martyrs often become depressed, or gain weight, as they are so unfulfilled. They live in a world with little freedom, even though it is usually self imposed.

If this is your life, take it back. Your partner needs the person he fell in love with. You are not doing him any favours by not being true to yourself. Whatever you are doing in your life, do it because you want to.

* * *

Meaghan was beautiful, slim and successful. She lived in a gorgeous home, with her lovely children and a kind, caring partner. She worked part-time, and was in my eyes, the epitome of a successful woman. But she had a dark secret. Underneath her attractive, competent exterior was a tired, worn out and overworked woman. She suffered from perfectionism in every area of her life. However that wasn't the problem.

Meaghan told me that she loved her husband, but was no longer 'in love' with her husband. This shocked me to the core, as they seemed like the perfect couple. He was handsome, had a great career, and she appeared to be the perfect, doting wife. They flirted with each other and seemed to get on famously. I was intrigued, confused and saddened. Yet after talking with Meaghan, I discovered she was just exhausted with her life. She was obsessed with her children's lives and maintaining her perfectly neat 'display home', and had subsequently worn-herself out. She was last on her list of priorities. She was neglecting herself, and consequently neglecting her husband, as she had nothing left to give. She was just 'going through the motions', rather than doing what made her feel alive. She was feeling numb inside from neglecting her needs for the sake of everyone else. As a result, she was losing her passion for life. She constantly strived to be the perfect employee, friend, neighbour, mother and wife. Yet she had forgotten one thing: she never did anything for herself. Naturally, when Meaghan's husband would ask her for sex, she would feel pressured and resentful. She saw sex as just another chore she had to do for someone else.

Eventually Meaghan ended up selling her house and moving. The change of house triggered a change of work and a complete change of attitude. When I last spoke to her she said, 'I love my husband, and I am in love with him'. What a fantastic turn around. Her sex life had also improved. She is finally living for herself, and not just everyone else. She is no longer being a martyr and is finally happy. Her happiness with her life has enabled her to participate fully in her marriage again.

* * *

Homework

If you love him,
but you're not *in love* with him

If this statement describes your feelings about your partner, try the following to turn it around:

- Don't be a martyr

- Treat him like a lover — not a brother

- Have some time without your spouse
  (Some distance can make the heart grow fonder)

- Start romancing and flirting with your partner again

- Do things for yourself, not everyone else all the time

- Reduce any resentment towards your partner

- Spend one night a week dating your partner.

- Make yourself happy

- Follow your passions.

- Make as many positive changes in your life as possible.

What are you *not* doing with your life?

If you don't know what you want out of life, ask yourself what would *you* want to do if you only had six months to live? How would you answer the following questions?

- Have you enjoyed quality time with your children and family?

- Have you loved deeply, every day?

- Have you accomplished all you set out to achieve in life so far?

- Have you participated in hobbies or sporting activities?

- Have you been on every holiday you wanted to take?

- Have you studied all the courses you wanted to study?

You and your partner are both individuals; you were born separately and will die at different moments.

You need to do what makes you happy, and your partner needs to do what makes him happy.

Allow enough breathing space for each of you to follow your own individual passions.

Step Three

Communicate well every day

A marriage is a friendship of the highest level. Just like any kind of friendship, a marriage only remains strong with regular communication.

Have daily chats

Daily, honest communication with your husband is essential in maintaining the emotional connection and keeping the friendship alive. These daily talks are a crucial part of a fantastic marriage. Think of them as the glue that keeps your relationship together, day after day, year after year. In this busy fast-paced world, it is so easy to neglect your partner and stop talking about the things that really matter. Make sure you and your partner keep the lines of communication open by having at least one stop-and-chat session per day. It's easy to drift apart from your partner. Don't let one day pass without talking.

Do you find your man needs 'unwind time'?

Interestingly, men speak approximately 7000 words per day, compared to woman, who speak approximately 22,000. What happens when he walks through the door after work, having spoken most of his words? He sits down to relax, and you walk up to him with your 19,500 un-spoken words. Sound familiar?

While you need to communicate well every day with your spouse, men seem to need 'space' when they get home from work. Many of the men I have spoken to said that their wives seem to pounce on them, and start talking constantly, as soon as they get home from work. All these men want to do is simply relax first, have a little peace, and then they will be mentally ready to discuss all the days events.

Be your partner's best friend

Aim to have as many 'cuppas' together as possible during the day or at night when the children are in bed. Find a quiet room with no distractions where you can sit and talk about your day. It is really sad when a couple spend days without talking.

Daily chats are the basis of all great friendships. A friendship evolves and changes over time, and just because you were best friends once does not mean you will stay best friends forever. Friendships need to be nurtured, especially the friendship with your lifelong partner.

Breakfast, Dinner and Bed Time

Breakfast: Life is hectic and busy. We all benefit from our morning chats with our partners. Can you get up that half hour earlier for a nice leisurely breakfast with your partner? If you can't have breakfast together, what about a coffee? One friend meets her husband every morning for coffee. How romantic is that?

Dinner Time: As often as possible, try to enjoy dinner with the whole family, without the TV on. It's a great opportunity for the family to get together and discuss the day at work, home or school. This is also the perfect time to raise any important issues that need to be discussed.

Bed Time: It is wonderful to go to bed with your partner every night. Beds are so much fun. Try to allow time for a little chat before sleeping. If this is not possible, due to work or other commitments, try to go to bed together at least a couple of times a week. Never going to bed at the same time is a tragedy. For some mysterious reason, going to bed together is such a bonding experience, especially if you talk, cuddle, kiss and tell each other how much you love each other, before going to sleep.

Know what you want

It's necessary to have an overall picture in your mind of the type of relationship you want with your partner. What do you expect from both your relationship and your partner? Do you expect to chat freely with him every day, about work and your lives? Do you expect your partner to share his feelings with you all the time? It may be easier if you bring to mind a happy couple you know, and model your expectations on their relationship. What qualities do they have in their partnership, which you would like in your own? Once you have a clear picture of what you want from your relationship, physically and emotionally, make sure you stay on track.

Don't settle for an average marriage

Are you settling for an average marriage? Too many women don't ask for what they want and instead become restless, resentful and bored with their partners. You continually need to ask for what you want and need from your relationship. If there is something wrong or something you want to pursue (like a gym membership or dancing classes), sit down and talk about it.

Don't settle for an average marriage when you can have a great marriage, just by discussing your needs. Sure, it's not possible to have an amazing relationship *all* the time. You will go through hard times, but you should feel like you are in a great relationship *most* of the time.

Be honest with yourself

If you can honestly admit to yourself what is not working in your relationship, you are one step closer to improving it. Before you can be honest with your partner, you need to be honest with yourself. If you lie to yourself all the time, you may lose sight of three very important things: who you are, what you want from your marriage and what you want from your life. It may help to start keeping a diary. By reading back over all your thoughts, emotions and desires, you will see a clearer picture of who you are and what you want in life. This will help you become more honest with yourself and your partner.

Be honest with your partner

In most cases, it's best to be honest with your partner. You will have a greater chance of being on the 'same wavelength' by understanding each other's challenges, decisions and emotions. Great friendships are built on sharing life's little details with each other.

There are some things, however, which you should not tell your partner. If you know that something trivial would upset him, then he may be better off not knowing. This is not to be confused with keeping a big secret from your partner. I try to keep my partner's stress to a minimum, so on the odd occasion I don't tell him stressful things. I usually tell him almost everything, but I certainly would not rush home and tell him that I'd just spent $124 on clothes, $27 on moisturizer and $85 on foils and a hair cut. Being a woman is expensive, and if he asks I'll tell him how much money I spent. But why stress him out unnecessarily? Being honest means telling your partner 'where you are at' in life. Exposing the deepest parts of your soul and sharing the kind of thoughts you would only share with your partner and best friend. Being honest is not holding back on the big things.

Do fun things together

When you start dating you normally do many fun or creative things with your partner. In the early stages of a marriage many couples still continue to do fun things together, such as finding the right appliances, choosing furniture, renovating, or gardening. Many couples continue this adventure together forever, working side by side in or outside the home. Some couples enjoy entertaining, having barbeques or throwing parties. Others play sport together or eat take-away and watch great DVDs. Many couples have family afternoons with their children on weekends. All these activities strengthen the bond and deepen the love between spouses. They can also increase your libido.

If you are in the habit of not doing things together on a weekly basis, you are headed for trouble. Many couples drift apart from each other because they don't do enjoyable things together regularly.

Laugh together

Laughing together is one of the greatest things you can do for your marriage. It's even great to laugh at each other, or at your children. As long as the laughter is not cruel, laughing at your spouse and teasing him is basically flirting and can spice up your relationship. Go through the television guide and circle all the comedies, so you can watch and enjoy them together. Laughter invigorates the mind and body and can even put you both in the mood for loving. So next time he does something ridiculously funny, don't be afraid to laugh your head off at him.

Just make sure you don't laugh at him while you are between the sheets. No man likes to be laughed at while he is performing unless he's a comedian.

Ask for what you want and need

One of the most common marital problems is each partner not communicating their needs to the other. He may think he's a great husband because he works hard, pays the bills and is faithful. She may think she's a great wife because the house is clean, the children are well looked after, and his sock drawer is full. Yet, these are *not* the key ingredients in passionate marriages.

Women want friendship, love and plenty of attention. They don't want a partner who simply gives them their wages, mows the lawn, services the car and then ignores them. Women are complicated. They crave friendship, intimacy, love and a deep connection with their partners, but they don't often explain this to them.

Men love a tidy house, but most wouldn't care less if they had to crawl over two baskets of unfolded washing to get to your naked body. Men are simple in their approach to marriage. They are highly practical and want to 'fix' the marriage if there are problems.

* * *

Roger, a friend of the family, was frustrated by his marriage problems. He did not understand why his wife was not happy, and his wife could not seem to convey to him what she needed, in order to be happy. Our conversation inspired me to write the following sample letters, showing both sides more clearly. These letters illustrate clearly the different expectations held by women and men, which are not often expressed.

To my wife

I know there is a problem. I just don't know what it is. I work hard and provide for the family. I think I'm a good Dad and husband. I just don't understand you anymore. I ask my mates and they say, 'All women are mad, can't live with 'em, can't live without 'em'. I can fix things at work. That's not complicated. Why is this relationship so damn complicated? To me, it's simple. I love you, so I married you. Marriage is forever. Of course, I'm not cheating on you! Cheating doesn't even cross my mind. Why are you so suspicious? Anyway, I'm always working, when could I possibly cheat? And speaking of problems, how come you used to want sex all the time, but now I'm the only one who wants it? You never chase me for sex. To me, the only problems are your lack of sex drive and your nagging. I don't know what you want anymore. I do try. I bought you flowers and took you on holidays. I don't want to end this. I don't want to start again. What am I dealing with? You're up and then you're down. What can I do to stop the shit from hitting the fan all the time? I need to fix this problem. I want to live in a peaceful house. I want to feel needed, especially by you. I work so hard to provide a roof over our heads. I promise I will do all I can to make this marriage work.

In desperate times change the above letter to suit your situation and give it to your wife.

To my husband

I am dealing with a problem that has been going on for months. I don't know how, but we seem to have drifted apart. I feel so lonely and so empty. I am sick and tired of fighting with you. I do appreciate that you provide for the family and you're a great father, but that's not the problem. The problem is our relationship. I find life so hard at times. I'm not just your wife; I'm also the mother of our children. I have to pay the bills, go shopping, cook the meals, do the housework and work part-time. Sometimes, I feel like I won't be able to get off the couch at the end of the day. And when things are really tough for me, and I just need some help from you, you tell me you have done everything you can because you've worked all day. My work never ends! I need more from you than just financial support. I want you to show me how much you love me every day. I want you to cuddle me anytime of the day or night and not just when you want sex. I want you to ask me what I need, so I can tell you that I am tired and need a shoulder to lean on. I may not get paid for my many hours of housework and caring for the children, but I desperately want to feel appreciated by you. I want to feel like you love, adore and understand me. Please spend a few minutes a day just listening to me talk about my thoughts and feelings. I understand my world is very different to yours and my concerns may seem trivial, but I just want to be heard. Please understand that you don't have to fix my problems, I just want to get them off my chest and share them with you. I really need you to be my friend for life. Underneath my bold exterior, I am fragile and I need your love and support (like when we were first married). I don't want to turn to any other man to feel special. I want to feel special by looking into your eyes and being held in your arms. I want attention every day. I also want you to know I am not like you; I don't feel like sex any time of the day or night, but I love romance, kissing, massages and passion. I would rather make

35

passionate love with you, than just 'lie there', so please be more romantic. Life's not always easy, but I want to be with you through it all. I want to adore and cherish you, so please don't pick on me for not being a size ten anymore. Whatever we face, we can face it together. I want to be your best friend.

In desperate times change to suit your situation and give it to your husband.

Homework

Keep communication flowing
Don't hold back

If you want to say something to your partner, say it. Get it off your chest. Don't wait a day, or even an hour, if you can help it. A problem shared is often a problem solved.

You have two choices:

1. Bottle your emotions inside and feel like you're going to explode.

2. Communicate how you feel, even if you face possible ridicule.

If there is anything that needs discussing such as the status of your relationship, the children, money problems, concerns about the neighbours or fears you are spending too much time apart, don't hesitate. As soon as possible say, 'We need to have a cuppa and chat about . . .', then sit down and start talking and listening.

You can avoid potential dramas by keeping the communication flowing between yourself and your spouse.

Step Four

Invest time and money in your relationship weekly

A marriage is just like a garden; neglect it, and it will die or become full of weeds. Both partners need to invest time in the marriage, for it to blossom.

Invest time in grooming

Try to make the effort to look good for your partner as often as you can. Your partner deserves to see you looking 'your best' at least once a week. You certainly don't need to walk around the house in tight jeans and low cut tops, with perfect hair and make-up all day and night. However, you should make the effort to look good most of the time. Naturally I emphasize putting that little extra effort into looking your best for your weekly date night (more about date night later).

Tracksuit wearers beware: If you need to exercise, tracksuits (jogging suits) are perfect for that, but unless you look sensational in a pair of tracksuit pants (some lucky women do), then wear them strictly for what they were designed for! If you want to gain weight easily, wear loose pants. If you only wear loose pants (like tracksuit pants), your clothes won't let you know if you've put on a kilo or two, whereas a pair of tight jeans definitely will. So think of those faithful jeans as the diet police and wear tracksuits only when cleaning the house or exercising.

Invest money in your relationship

You need to make a financial commitment to your marriage that incorporates weekly activities. Even if you have huge debts, aim to budget for your special children's night and a date night at the very least. You may not be able to afford to go away together on weekends or out to dinner, but at least you will spend two great nights a week with your partner and family.

Life's not just about working to pay bills — it's about creating happy memories too.

Have a weekly family afternoon

No matter how busy you are, try to find time to do something fun with the family on a weekend afternoon. Go for a family drive, or a bike ride in the park, have a picnic by a lake, or watch a video together on a rainy day. Perhaps the family could have a weekend away at a tourist park. It's amazing how affordable and tranquil one weekend away with the family can be.

Add your family activities to the budget. The family that plays together, stays together.

Make your partner a priority

Some couples have their priorities 'out of whack', and wonder why their marriages are failing. If you invest time and money in your home, the latest furniture, the new car, and all the latest brand name clothing, and completely forget about spending time and money on your marriage, wouldn't that be unbalanced?

Even the most stable marriage can end in divorce if both partners don't invest time and money in their marriage.

* * *

Leanne appeared to have a close relationship with her husband. They would spend every Friday night together with the family. They were happy, until they purchased a more expensive house. Leanne and her partner increased their work hours, so they could pay for their dream home. They both worked many hours and stopped devoting time to each other. Leanne started socializing with her work colleagues more and more, and over the next two years, the marriage started to disintegrate. From the outside it was very obvious that Leanne's partner was no longer an important priority in her life. She would socialize with friends and workmates, but push her partner aside. Eventually Leanne and her partner drifted apart. Leanne then became close to a work mate and started to fall in love with him. Leanne is now divorced.

Who knows what was meant to be? All I can be sure of is: If you don't nourish your relationship, it will die.

* * *

Anthony and his wife were very focused on their financial goals. Anthony worked extremely hard so that he could provide an outstanding lifestyle for his wife and family. He worked full-time during the week and also held down a part-time job on the weekends. He spent the little time he had off renovating the family home. His wife would stay home and look after the children.

Their relationship began to change. Anthony was concerned because his wife was becoming emotionally distant, and was spending many hours in the bedroom on her computer, but he did nothing. Then one day his wife told him that she was leaving him for a man who lived overseas, who she had been communicating with over the internet.

Sadly, while Anthony had been spending many hours working two jobs and renovating their family home, she had been falling in love with her internet lover. Anthony was devastated and destroyed.

Most of Anthony's time was being spent on his work, his second job and the renovations. Unfortunately, his marriage failed as because he did not invest enough time in his relationships with both his wife and his children.

As with standard affairs, internet affairs usually begin because of emptiness in the heart and/or life of the person.

Homework

Have a weekly date night

- Break up your busy week with a night of relaxation, entertainment and romance for yourself and your partner. Date night is your chance to snuggle up on the couch with your partner, cuddle, talk and totally enjoy each other, every week.

- Choose a night when you are both free every week, and call this night 'Date Night'. For this one night, don't think about cooking, cleaning or paying bills. This night belongs to you and your partner. Get dressed up in your favourite, most sexy outfits, and go out and buy your favourite takeaway meal and hire a couple of great DVDs. Enjoy your takeaway dinner with the family and then set up the TV for the children (or put them to bed), and go into another part of the house for your quality time with your spouse. Tell your children that Saturday night is 'Mummy and Daddy's night'. If they behave, they can stay up and watch their DVD. But if they misbehave, they will go straight to bed.

- So light the fire (or put the heater on), kick back and have some drinks from the bar (or fridge), relax and talk with your partner, child free.

- If you are serious about transforming your relationship, start dating your partner this weekend. Make date night a weekly ritual.

Step Five

Stop finding fault and start praising

Focus on your partner's strengths and not their weaknesses. The more you think about their positives, the more positives you will see, which will make your relationship stronger.

Praise your partner daily

Have you ever noticed that after purchasing a car, all you see on the road are the same model of car that you just bought? This is exactly how your mind works. Whatever you choose to focus on occupies your mind.

The more you praise your partner, the better your relationship will be. Praise is a powerful motivating factor. You can improve almost anything about your partner just by praising him. When you tell your partner you appreciate what he does, it's only natural he will want to do it more often. Praising is cherishing your partner (as promised in many wedding vows). You are creating an impact on your partner's life every day, so why not make it a positive one.

I praise my partner all the time for being a great friend, a fantastic lover and a wonderful father to our children. I also praise him for being dedicated to his work, helping around the house and being supportive of my life choices. While I'm praising him for all his strengths, he just seems to grow stronger and stronger. It is a win-win situation.

A partner who is praised often will become a more confident, successful and loving partner. Watch this miracle occur in your marriage when you start praising daily.

Try not to criticize your partner

When you have been married for a while, it's easy to fall into the habit of treating your partner badly and losing respect for him. Many women have treated their partners poorly for so long they end up thinking of them as less than real men. Eventually, these women see only their partners' negative points and their partners simply cannot do anything to please them. It is a common scenario to hear a woman publicly criticize her partner, and her partner simply put up with it and not defend himself against the put downs and degrading comments. The man doesn't appear to show any backbone or have an ounce of self respect by allowing his partner to talk to him disrespectfully.

If your partner is victimizing you, stand on your own two feet and refuse to accept their continual criticisms. If you are inclined to put your partner down a lot, you can reverse this destructive pattern.

Once you start focusing on your partner's good points, and start praising him more, you'll find you criticize him less. As your focus changes, your whole attitude towards your partner will change for the better.

Nitpickers Beware!

Expecting your husband to do the following will lead to disappointment.

Most men do not:

Like being nagged
Change the toilet roll
Remember to put the bins out
Have the ability to read your mind
Keep towels and tea towels straight
Feel the need to talk to you constantly
Cuddle you without being asked all the time
Bring you flowers or chocolate for no reason
Pick up coffee cups and place them on the sink
Clean up the house or do dishes when baby-sitting
Want to tell you every single detail about their day
Consistently put dirty clothes in the dirty washing basket
Ensure the children are clean and nicely dressed when out

45

It is a waste of time, and a thorn in the side of your marriage, if you nit pick your husband. Accept that he is not like you. He has different redeeming qualities; these are what you should be focusing on. No woman can be happily married if she is nitpicking her husband.

Stop complaining and start outsourcing

Your partner's role is to love you and be your best friend, so try to work with his faults, instead of telling everyone else about them. If you are married to a workaholic, and he's too busy to mow the lawns, don't get mad; instead hire a person to mow them, or do it yourself. These days most jobs in and around the house can be outsourced. A girlfriend taught me this lesson. Her husband couldn't fix a thing, so what did she do? She bought her own tools and did most of the jobs herself.

Do you have your own tools? I finally have my own screwdriver set, which is a must for replacing batteries in children's toys. I bought them because I could never find my partner's screwdrivers.

Avoid bitching sessions

At all costs, avoid getting into bitching sessions about your partner. It may seem like fun to make your partner the brunt of your jokes, but once you start bitching about him, you are heading for trouble. Next time you start to bitch about your partner, pay attention to that horrible feeling in the pit of your stomach. That gut feeling is telling you that what you are doing is not right. While you are sitting there complaining, you are consciously and subconsciously focusing on your partner's negative points. Your friends could make matters worse by adding a few negative remarks like, 'Oh God. You deserve a medal for putting up with him.' This is only going to make you even more bitter or resentful.

Some women even bitch about their partners for attention. They love to shock their friends with stories about their husband's terrible behaviour. The sad reality is women who complain about their partners for the shock value, are simultaneously destroying their marriages.

No husband is perfect, after all. He cannot possibly be an awesome father to your children, romance you constantly, do all the housework, earn $95,000 a year and take out the garbage. Something has to give.

The grass is not always greener

Be careful not to compare your spouse with your friends' partners too much, as many people exaggerate when it comes to their relationships, income and sex lives. Women who brag about their perfect husbands are often just trying to make themselves feel superior by making *you* feel inferior. This sort of behaviour creates unnecessary jealousy. They may brag about how perfect and romantic their husband is; how they do all the cooking and shopping and read to the children every night. This type of friend, who brags about their perfect marriage, can cut to the very soul of a person having marriage trouble.

Bear in mind that many couples don't show the world a true glimpse of their marriage. They may appear to have a happy marriage, yet they could be living in an emotional vacuum. Unhappily married couples often put on a happy front. If they can't be happy in the relationship, then at least they can look happy.

When our marriage was at its worst, my partner and I would go out to a family function and put on a happy front. It wasn't until we got in the car that the arguments, or silence, would begin again.

Your relationship is all about you and your partner. As long as you are both meeting most of each other's needs, that is fantastic. Other people's lives may seem flawless, but that is because you haven't lived with them in their house, day after day, month after month.

Your marriage may be a whole lot better than you thought. The grass is usually not greener on the other side of the fence. It is often an illusion.

My story — over a decade ago

Our marriage was struggling. One of the issues contributing to our marriage problems was my bad attitude towards my husband. I was just so critical. He worked extremely hard at his job and always tried to create ways of making more money for the family. He was faithful, worked tirelessly around the garden and even helped me and my covers band by being our sound technician at gigs. Yet, I would constantly think negative thoughts about him. I would focus on all his negative points and annoying habits. I was hardly aware of his positive points anymore. I felt resentful that he would rarely take me out for dinner or help with the housework. I would obsess about him leaving his tools, coffee cups, and just about every-thing else he picked up, all around the house, backyard and shed. Almost every night, I'd feel resentful about going to bed alone because he was working on the computer.

The more I thought about his bad habits, the more I would see. It was a vicious circle.

My story — now

Funnily enough, my partner still leaves coffee cups all around the house, office and shed, he still works on the computer every night and still doesn't like to go out to dinner much. Sure, he has improved, and sometimes does the vacuuming and dishes these days. However, the major change is that I am no longer a resentful wife. I focus on his good points instead of his bad points. I not only accept his annoying habits; I usually make allowances for them. I will go out for dinner with girlfriends instead of my partner. I enjoy going to bed and reading motivational books while I'm waiting for him to get off the computer. I've even grown accustomed to my role of 'coffee cup fetcher' and have found a nice big plastic container in which to throw all his tools that I still find lying around the house, shed and backyard.

Which one of us has changed over the past decade? Was it my attitudes that changed, or did my partner improve as a husband? Well, my partner still has negative points and annoying habits, but because I'm not dwelling on them anymore, our marriage has been great. I am also happier and more content. Besides that, what woman enjoys being a nag all the time?

Now I constantly think about what a great husband I have. I am not trying to change him anymore. He has a supportive and loving wife, who praises him more and criticizes less, and he feels secure enough to be himself.

Homework

Never complain about your partner
to other people

- Never let your anger and resentment build to the point where you need to complain about your partner to every person you meet.

- Fault finding and nitpicking are dangerous habits.

- Complaining to others about your partner is extremely destructive.

- If you have a complaint about your partner, tell him!

- It's the quickest way to resolve a problem.

- When you complain about your partner to everyone, you're effectively turning a molehill into a mountain.

- The problem just gets bigger in your mind.

Step Six

Plan the Romance

All wonderful marriages have romance. When you start dating romance happens naturally, but after a while, you need to plan for it.

Plan the romance

Every marriage should have at least a little romance, whether it is watching the sun set on the beach, or spending a night away together. It is possible to have a marriage filled with romance, even on a small budget.

Ask your partner to go through the following romantic suggestions with you. They are simply ideas, so that you can start your own romantic 'to do' list:

- Give your partner flowers or chocolates.
- Your partner could prepare a special 'mystery' candlelit dinner for you both, while you wait in the lounge room with a nice bottle of wine. (Don't peep. It's all about the surprise.)
- Have a night away from the children at a classy hotel in the city.
- On a warm night sneak outside into the garden while the children are asleep and enjoy a cocktail in the moonlight together.
- One Saturday afternoon, be spontaneous by packing up and going away for the remainder of the weekend.
- Prepare a Japanese style meal. Eat it together sitting on the lounge floor with your food laid out on the coffee table. Complete the look with tea candles and Japanese decorations.
- Surprise your partner with a limousine trip to your local casino. Dress to impress.
- Constantly flirt and tease your partner every chance you get.
- Enjoy a family picnic by a lake.
- Have as many quiet breakfasts together as you possibly can.

- To set the mood for romance, play love songs on the stereo and place tea candles around the living area, bedroom or bathroom.
- On your wedding anniversary relive your wedding night again at the same venue.
- Have fun nights in bed watching great movies together.
- Buy your man underwear in the new appealing styles.
- Dress up for each other. When he comes home from work surprise him by being dressed as a French maid, or whatever else takes your fancy.
- Plan and book a surprise romantic weekend away.
- *Suggestions for hubby:* Buy sexy lingerie for your wife. If you're shy, buy online. Buy jewellery, most women love it.

Look ready for romance

Grooming is vital! Do you want your man to continually look at you with lust? Are you putting effort into doing your hair and make-up, wearing perfume and dressing stylishly for him, as often as possible? Isn't your man worth a little extra effort? And if you're like most women, you simply love clothes shopping. Now if there is ever a reason to go clothes shopping, it is to impress your man! To be ready for romance, you must have sexy clothing to wear on all occasions. You will need a combination of sexy tops, tight jeans, and great skirts, to look the best you can for your partner.

Clothes make the man

If your partner doesn't mind, go out and buy some sexy looking outfits for him. Then whenever he puts them on, you should be more attracted to him. It's also in your best interest to check his wardrobe, every now and then, so that you can remove those clothes that don't look any good on your partner, anymore. Murphy's Law dictates that any item of clothing in the cupboard that you don't like will end up on him when you least expect it — like at your next work party. So throw out, or give away, the old fashioned shirts, daggy t-shirts and holey jeans (you may need to check with him first, as some guys are amazingly attached to their old rags). Then fill his wardrobe with clothes that you love. He's your man, so dress him the way you want. Hopefully he won't mind. On the other hand, if he has better taste in clothes than you do, let him organize your wardrobe and take you shopping instead.

Dress sexy and you'll feel sexy

If you are struggling to get your sex drive back, dress sexy more often. You are more likely to feel sexy if you are wearing a great bra, alluring underwear and a tight, low cut top. Buy sexy underwear (if you don't already have a drawer full), and wear them on Date Night. If you're feeling sexy, you're more likely to have a night of hot passion! Do it for your man and for yourself.

Does hubby prefer the natural look?

When most women start dating their partners, they are usually well groomed and spend lots of time and effort making sure they look their best. Most men find this extra effort appealing. Nevertheless, over the years, some husbands tell their wives they look better without the makeup, great hairstyles and sexy clothes. They tell their wives that they prefer the 'natural look'. These wives then end up looking totally different to the woman their husband first felt attracted to. This whole scenario is bizarre. After gradually changing the whole look of their wives over time, many of these men enthusiastically perve at and lust after, women who have the same well groomed, sexy appearance their wife had. Why would they do this? Could it be insecurity? After all some men cannot handle having an attractive partner for fear she may be stolen away. Not all men are like this, thank goodness!

If it makes you feel better to put the effort into your appearance then at least do it for yourself.

Flirt with your partner daily

Everyone needs to flirt, and it makes for a better marriage when you flirt often with your partner. When you flirt with, or tease your partner, you usually feel more passionate and alive. And while you're spending your days and nights flirting with your partner, you are less likely to feel the need to go and flirt with other men.

If you're not flirting with your partner the desire to flirt with other men is likely to be stronger. All affairs start with one thing — flirting. It's just so much easier (and guilt free), to flirt with your partner instead. So go up to your partner and whisper naughty little suggestions in his ear anytime, night or day.

Is your bedroom like a hotel room?

I went to my best friend's home and looked into her bedroom. I was amazed. It looked just like a hotel room. Her bedroom was decorated with expensive bedroom furniture, nice lamps and a gorgeous 'classy hotel' type of bedspread. It really made me feel like I was on holidays and her bedroom was the expensive hotel suite.

That was all the inspiration I needed to makeover our bedroom. Not long after that day, my partner and I did our bedroom up to look exactly the way we had always wanted it to. We finally purchased a new bedroom suite, lamps, an elegant doona cover and multiple pillows and throw cushions. We also painted a feature wall in a great cappuccino colour.

Our thirteenth wedding anniversary was approaching, so I went on the internet to find a hotel room to stay at in the city, and guess what? Something unbelievable happened. I could not find a room in any four or five star hotel that looked as classy and cosy as our bedroom at home. After much consideration, I thought it would be more fun if we just bought a DVD player instead, set the TV and DVD player up in the bedroom, and stayed in our own 'hotel room' for the night.

Ever since that night, we simply love spending time in our bedroom. It is our favourite room in the house. We are happier and our life has more romance, due to our hotel-style bedroom.

* * *

Interview with a 'spy for women'

Despite my best efforts, over a six month period, I found it impossible to find a man, who had an extra-marital affair, and would talk to me about it.

I needed someone 'on the inside'. So, in an effort to understand why some men are unfaithful to the wives they love, I interviewed a woman who spent the past twenty years working in a male dominated profession. *She,* like all women, was happy to talk.

In your opinion, what percentage of the men you work with are unfaithful and what percentage are loyal, faithful guys?

I'd say thirty percent of guys I work with are decent guys. However, half of these thirty percent end up being unfaithful eventually if they are neglected by their wives.

Wow, that's a really high percentage. You are saying that only fifteen percent of the guys you work with remain faithful. I can understand the players being unfaithful (especially as women often throw themselves men in uniform), but why do the decent guys stray?

Women need to face the facts: guys start to climb the walls without sex, especially if they are fit and healthy like these guys. Sure, a man can wait a few months without sex if his wife has had a baby, but if she continually refuses to have sex with him, he will eventually find a girlfriend on the side. Most guys don't usually start an affair as soon as their wives have a baby and start neglecting them. They normally soul-search and agonize for months, or even years, before they have sex on the side. These decent guys are basically extremely loyal, but have been pushed to the brink after being constantly rejected by their wives.

So, are you saying a lot of your workmates have a girlfriend on the side — a mistress? Why don't they just leave their wives?

Yes, most of the guys that are unfaithful have girlfriends. Many men stay with their wives because they love their wives, they just have sex elsewhere. Many men stay with their wives because they love the children so much that they don't want to leave, so they keep seeing a girlfriend on the side and stay in the marriage.

Can you give me an example of one of these decent guys who has been unfaithful, so I can better understand why?

Jimmy was married for nine years. He has three children. His wife gave him less and less sex after each child. He truly loved and worshipped his wife. He eventually got a girlfriend and after four years, left his wife to be with his lover. His girlfriend knew about his wife, but continued the relationship. It's amazing how many women out there are happy to have a relationship with a married man. Jimmy was the faithful type and for so many years he tried to be loyal, but he cracked under the pressure.

Tell me about the players (as you call them), the over-sexed, highly flirtatious and often unfaithful guys. I call these types of guys 'bulls'.

These guys pick up regardless of their looks. There are always girls out there who will hit on a man in uniform, no matter how ugly the guy is. They don't seem to feel any shame or guilt.

Have you ever known a player to be faithful?

No. I have met some of their partners and it doesn't matter how hot their ladies are, players will be unfaithful. I have never known a player be faithful.

What advice have you got for married women?

Be honest and open-minded with your partner. Try new things in the bedroom, make them happy. Buy lingerie and try kinky stuff. A happy, satisfied decent guy will generally not stray.

Don't push your husband aside. There are plenty of women out there who will be nice to them and have sex with them, if you won't.

Homework

Do up your bedroom together

Visit display houses and find a nice colour scheme to paint your master bedroom.

Keep checking the catalogues for manchester sales and buy yourself a classy doona cover when you can.

Give your marriage a boost by doing up your bedroom together!

Keep it tidy, romantic and ready for intimacy at all times.

Step Seven

Restore the passion

Each time you make love, your souls touch. Woven into these precious moments, is the glue that helps keep you both together, forever.

Step Seven

Part A:

Problems in the bedroom

Married women and sex

When most women get married they are full of passion for their husbands, but after the children are born and their lives get busier, many women end up feeling that sex is no longer an important priority.

Many of the women I have spoken with complained about their lack of sex drives, or that they generally have less interest in their partners sexually. Most of these women said they were usually too exhausted by the end of the day for sex. Some even complained that they felt so resentful when their partners pressured them to have sex, that they didn't feel attracted to their partners anymore. Some mentioned that their spouses rushed foreplay or were unadventurous and boring in the bedroom. Many women complained that they were sick of their partners nagging them all the time for sex. These women feel sex has become just another chore.

While I have also spoken to many women who really enjoy sex, I have spoken with very few women who simply can't get enough sex with their husbands.

Let's have a look at the differences between the male and female approach to sex.

Married men and sex

Men usually have a higher sex drive than women. Obviously this can, and does, cause problems. Men can have a tendency to feel like sex at any time of the day or night. A man may be aroused by a quick sexual thought, a word, an advertisement on TV, you bending over the dishwasher, or just plain sexual energy. Lust can be very instinctive for men. They can feel in the mood for loving at any moment without any apparent reason or conscious thought.

Also, unlike women, a man's sexual appetite doesn't necessarily change when the status of his emotional relationship changes.

Differing sexual appetites

A woman's sex drive is more closely linked to her emotions. Her sex drive is linked to the status of her emotional connection with her spouse and many other possible complications in her life. When she was single and had more time, energy and focus, her sex drive was most likely a lot higher.

A woman's sexual appetite is likely to be hindered if:

she has too many things on her mind
she does not feel close to her spouse
she is having problems at work
she is worried about money
the children are still awake
the bedroom is messy
she is feeling resentful
hubby smells of beer
she has a house guest
she is feeling insecure
she is feeling jealous
the house is messy
she is hormonal
she is feeling fat
she is upset
or
she
is
just worn out and tired.

A man's sexual appetite is likely to be hindered if:
he is extremely unhappy in his work
he is depressed or
he is drunk.

Men and women are different

Men have been designed to ensure that the human race continues i.e. by having lots of sex and fathering children. Women have been designed to make sure the human race survives i.e. by looking after the children, the home and the husband.

These fundamental differences cause problems in many marriages. At the end a busy day, the wife wants to sit down and rest (tired from running around after the family all day), but hubby may want to have sex (to ensure the survival of the human race). Does this sound familiar?

Are you a habitual leg crosser?

Lack of interest in your partner's sexual advances is likely to be caused by other issues in your life and relationship. If you address these issues, the passion should return. Ask your partner if he thinks you reject his advances all the time. If he says yes, then try to change your priorities.

Men desperately need to feel important and wanted in their world, especially by their wives and families. Most of all, they need to feel that their wives appreciate them and find them sexually attractive. If you reject his advances all the time, you are literally chipping away at the very foundations of his being. Did you reject his advances all the time when you first met? No? Well, is it fair that you do so now?

If you were sexually attracted to him when you started dating, but are no longer attracted to him, this passion can return. Amazing chemistry between two people does not disappear; it simply dies down with distractions.

8 Reasons why you may be rejecting him:

1. Putting your children and housework first?
Many married women are putting their children (and their children's extra curriculum activities), the housework and work, before sex. Striving to be the perfect mother and housewife seems to be the number one reason that wives are rejecting their husbands. It's really important to make sure you keep your priorities in the right order. Do you have an over-scheduled lifestyle with no time allocated for sex? If so, then get out of the kitchen and into the bedroom. Is it possible to re-organize your busy schedule so that you can either accommodate your man during the day or go to bed with him a little earlier? Ask your man if he would prefer to have sex more often or a full underwear drawer every day.

2. Do you feel resentment towards your partner?
Resentment is a common reason why women are losing sexual interest in their husbands. So men, if you want more sex, you will need to find out if, or why, your wife is feeling resentful towards you. If you are treating your wife like a prisoner, controlling her, not helping her with the housework or children, not listening to her and not being her best friend, how can you expect her to be your adoring sex kitten?

3. Are you on the contraceptive pill?
Research shows that the pill can reduce a woman's sex drive. When a woman takes the pill, the hormones oestrogen and

progestin down-regulate your body's hormonal balance. According to studies performed by Boston University Medical Centre, USA, the pill raises the level of Sex Hormone Binding Globulin (SHBG), which blocks the production of testosterone. Lowered testosterone in women can result in lowered libido.

There is also new research on the internet (from various sources) about the possible long term side effects on women's sex drives who currently take the pill, and even for those who have stopped.

Please consult your doctor if you are experiencing low libido. You may benefit from changing brands or stopping the pill all together. Some women do not experience a decrease in libido, at all, from taking the pill. Some pills can actually boost testosterone levels. However, I encourage you to do your own research on the internet. After all, it is your body, your sex drive, and your life.

4. Do you have a poor body image?

Have you gained weight over the years? Do you feel like you are not sexy anymore? Do you feel ashamed to be naked in front of your partner? Don't worry, you normally look at your body with a more critical eye than him, as you're judging and he's usually lusting. If you don't mention the stretch marks and cellulite to him, he probably won't even notice them! (Maybe it's because he's too busy looking at the rude bits). Understand that when you look in the mirror, you are most likely subconsciously comparing yourself with all the size 8 models and stars in the latest gossip magazine. (And if it makes you feel any better, the average woman in Australia is about size 14). Your hubby is more likely to be lusting after you when he sees you naked, than mentally measuring the size of your thighs! Most men worship the female body and are attracted to their wives, even if their wives have put on 10 kilos since they married. He's probably not perfect either. I'm sure he's put on a little padding around the waist himself.

5. Dry spell or sexual drought?

It's not unusual for couples to go through times when they don't feel like having sex for days, or even weeks, at a time. Your sex drive is linked to your energy reserves and if you don't have a lot of energy, then it can affect your sex drive dramatically. Sex is just like any other habit. Sometimes you want sex constantly and other times you don't seem to care for it at all. Dry spells are normal. Don't worry about it, unless the dry spell is extremely long and becomes a drought!

6. Stressed about work or money?

Are you overworked, tired or stressed by your job? This is a common cause of reduced sex drives, especially in men. Unhappiness at work, work related stress or depression can lower a man's libido. Most men find their libido also decreases as a result of financial strain.

7. Is life too busy for sex?

If you have a lot of time for yourself and hardly any stress in your life, you will find that you have more energy. Having more energy usually results in a higher sex drive. Try to free your life up so that you have a little more you time, and a little more energy for sexual romps around the house!

8. Is friendship missing from your relationship?

It's often due to emotional, rather than physical, issues that are causing married women to want less sex. Why? Because women usually need a strong friendship with their partners in order to feel sexually attracted to them. No woman wants to have sex with her husband if she is constantly fighting with, or feeling disconnected from him. If more husbands could truly understand that the quality of the friendship they have with their wives, has a huge bearing on their wives enthusiasm in bed, then more men would go to work in the morning with smiles on their faces.

Note to hubby: A proven way to get your wife in the mood for loving is a shopping spree (without the children). This works a treat for most women. If you want a hot night of passion, tell your wife to have some retail therapy. Most women feel sexy and relaxed after a shopping spree on clothes and lingerie or when they have simply had some quality time without the children. You may prefer to organize some pampering, quiet reading or relaxing time for her instead. The aim is for your wife to feel relaxed and stress free because women feel more in the mood for loving when they are relaxed.

Sexual frustration in men

If hubby wants to have sex all the time, but to no avail, he may become sexually frustrated. Sexual frustration brings with it some pretty unpleasant side effects. This frustration tends to make men agitated or aggressive. It may cause hubby to make nasty comments, start fights, get angry and throw tantrums or even sulk.

A man's need for sex is just like any other physical need such as eating, drinking or sleeping. It is a normal bodily function of men to crave sex. So if your hubby starts getting grumpy for no apparent reason, ask yourself, 'Has it been a while since you last fogged up the bedroom windows?'

Sexual frustration in women

Women's bodies, and hormones, are so different to men's. Consequently, most women don't experience the same level of sexual craving that men experience. Only a small percentage of women have very high sex drives just like men. They understand how men feel as they have experienced similar sexual frustration. However, most women cannot relate to the sexual frustration that many men experience.

Don't just lie there

A fantastic sex life starts with you wanting to have sex. I am not encouraging you to stop having sex with your partner — just make sure you are aroused first. Then sex will be a satisfying and enjoyable experience for you both and you will want to have sex more often.

It's an extremely common problem in marriage for wives to become sexually disinterested in their husbands. A number of women I have spoken to said that they only have sex with their husbands, so their husbands don't hassle them anymore. They admitted they were no longer attracted to their husbands. Some even seemed confused as to how a woman could remain attracted to their husbands after marriage and having children.

The point these women were missing is this: women who feel obliged to lie down and have sex (without foreplay) when asked, are doing themselves and their partners no favours. Over time, if they keep having 'boring sex' (without arousal or enjoyment) they will loose sexual interest in their husbands permanently. No wife should just lay there and submit to sex as if she is performing a service. Surely, your husband would prefer you to enthusiastically enjoy sex? And while not every sexual encounter will be amazing, *both* partners should enjoy the experience.

Every boring sexual encounter that you have with your partner is a nail in the coffin of your sex life and your marriage.

Men need to chase

Men do love being chased (sexually) from time to time, but no man likes to be hounded, nagged, criticized and winged at, especially when it comes to sex.

From time to time I meet women who seem to be constantly chasing their partners for sex. These women have higher sex drives than their partners. They dress up, chase, nag, threaten and complain that their partners do not have sex often enough with them.

While it must be frustrating for these women, they are missing a fundamental point: Men need to chase. They are cavemen after all, and as far as you go back in history, it's natural for a man to chase a woman. If you run around chasing him all the time for sex, you are stripping him of his instinctive urge to chase you.

So what do you do? Well, do what my best friend suggested. Act as if you don't want sex. You still dress up sexy for him, but remain aloof. Act as if you are not interested at all. This really works!

If you are a sex starved, hot blooded woman, who happens to be married to a man who rarely seems to want sex, try being more subtle in your seduction techniques. Let him think that he is chasing you, for a change, and see if you end up having sex more often. Often men find 'the thought of sex' more sexually appealing when it is elusive, and they think they have no chance.

You can't change the programming of man. Men need to run after, and catch, their lovers. If you run after him too often, you will scare him away. He needs to be the man.

Homework

Wives who neglect their husbands

Wives who are guilty of sexually neglecting their husbands need to be punished. Punishment to fit the crime:

1. Grab your man.
2. Throw him on the bed.
3. Force yourself on him.
4. Worship him.
5. Ravish him for a change.
6. Repeat every 30 days.

A change is as good as a holiday. Start chasing him for a change — he will love it!

* * *

Rated R for eRotic

Do you want to drive him wild?

If you haven't already, ask him if wants a sex show for one. You could touch yourself, or even masturbate, in front of him. This will definitely fog up the bedroom windows!

Step Seven

Part B:

Ideas & Suggestions

Praise — Make your man feel like a stud

The most important ingredient in creating your own personal love machine is: PRAISE. You have a responsibility as a woman, and as a wife, to make your man feel like a stud. If you constantly tell your partner 'oh, that felt great', 'can you do that again?' and 'you're amazing' during and after sex, your lover will improve unbelievably! Try it and see for yourself. As long as you are sincere, the more you tell your lover how great he is, the better he will become.

Some women don't praise their partners because they are afraid he'll 'become such an expert in the bedroom that he'll rush off and sleep with other women'. This is ridiculous! If you never praise him, your partner will loose confidence. A lover lacking confidence will be too scared to experiment with new ways to arouse and satisfy you, so everybody looses.

Appreciate and praise what he does as often as possible. Treat your husband like a sex God, from this day on!

Show him what you want

When you first start having sex with your partner he is like a blank canvas and you are the artist. You need to show him what you want and enjoy. Over time, you should tell your spouse everything that turns you on and everything you want him to do for you. If he's not good in bed, and you're not feeling satisfied by him, maybe he just doesn't spend time on all the things that turn you on. If you don't show him what you want, then how can you expect him to be the lover of your dreams?

Train your man to be the type of lover that you want, then you'll want more sex and he will be happy. He needs to know everything that drives you wild so that he can satisfy you, over and over again. Don't be scared to ask for what you want and your nights will become hotter and hotter!

If you have fantasies (like being handcuffed to the bed and teased), it's in your best interest to explore these fantasies together. Ask him if you want him to be rougher, or if you want to try a new position. If you don't ask, you may end up unsatisfied and wandering forever. Ask and you shall receive.

Foreplay makes *all* the difference

While sex seems to be mostly about the orgasm for a man, it's more often about the foreplay for a woman. Why? Well, considering many women don't even have orgasms during sexual intercourse, foreplay is far more critical for sexual satisfaction. Also, a woman's orgasms are usually more intense during sex, and more frequent, as a result of longer foreplay. So, if you want more foreplay, then simply ask for more. A quick two minute grope under the sheets is *not* enough time for most women to become fully aroused, and it is not enough time to prepare most women's bodies for multiple orgasms.

Not in the mood? Try a little O.F.F.

If you are tired and don't feel like sex at the end of the day, try a little O.F.F. (Obligation Free Foreplay). This works like magic for couples who are not having a lot of sex. How does it work? Well, let's say that you have had a really busy day with the children, gone shopping, cooked dinner, cleaned the kitchen, put a load of washing on, put away two baskets of ironing, read a bedtime story to the children and finally thrown yourself on the bed in sheer exhaustion. In walks hubby. He sees you lying on the bed and gets that familiar glint in his eye. You could tell him to get lost or you could turn things around with a little O.F.F. You could suggest that he massages your back or feet, or just cuddle and kiss you for a while (whatever you find relaxing and sexy). The point you need to make is that you can say NO.

O.F.F. is just a way of being pampered that may possibly lead to sex, with the option of saying no. Most of the time, you are likely to become aroused from the pampering. So once again, everyone wins; you will be pampered more and he will be rejected less.

Standard Foreplay vs Advanced Foreplay

There are two types of foreplay that can turn an uninterested wife into the lover she once was. Only one involves touching.

1. Standard foreplay — (Touching):
   Sweet-talking, kissing, caressing and all the usual stuff.

2. Advanced foreplay — (No touching):
   Many tired and overworked women become sexually aroused watching their partners do the dishes, helping with the children or helping with other household chores. The highest form of advanced foreplay involves a romantic dinner with the preparation and tidying up taken care of by hubby. Try it, and see how you go.

Having sex is like eating a nice meal

Think of sex as food for a moment. You feel like eating more when you smell food cooking. Similarly, you feel like sex more when you're aroused by foreplay. When you go to an expensive restaurant you can smell all the delicious food around you while you are waiting for your meal. When you eventually eat, you enjoy the meal even more, as you are hungrier than when you first walked in.

Imagine then, if you walked in the door of the restaurant and the waiter sat you down within a minute and said, 'Eat, eat, you have to finish this meal within five minutes'. Even worse, imagine you went to the restaurant twice a week and every time you go, you are ordered to sit and eat the meal immediately. Pretty soon you would stop wanting to go to that restaurant.

Sex is the same. If it is rammed down your throat (pardon the pun) two or three times a week, particularly if you are not aroused by great foreplay (smelling the food), then you have less chance of enjoying mind blowing sexual encounters.

Sex is all about give and take

Sex is all about taking turns: you giving him pleasure, him giving you pleasure, and you both pleasing each other. Try having a night occasionally where your partner receives all the pleasure from you. Then another time, it's your turn to receive all the pleasure from him. Ultimately, you should both feel like you are being pleasured and satisfied by each other most of the time. Variety adds to the enjoyment.

There is more to life than missionary

Your first sexual position may have been missionary (man on top and woman on her back). However, if that is the only position you are doing, you will be having a very dull sex life. To increase your chance of orgasms and pleasure, you need to experiment with a multitude of positions to find out what you both enjoy. If you want to learn more about the choices available to you, there are many books and instructional videos available.

Four basic types of sex

When you first started having sex, you may have thought that there was only one type of sex. However, if you think of sex as four basic types, it will make your sex life more balanced and enjoyable.

1. Sex
Basic sex is a very primal act. It is mostly about sexual satisfaction. It's something that can be performed with minimal emotional and spiritual connection. It is mostly about sexual satisfaction and the climax.

2. Making Love
Making love is all about kissing, caressing, holding each other closely, tenderness, passion and most importantly, the deep connection between two people, both emotionally and spiritually. The connection is at its deepest when looking into each other's eyes, while enjoying explosive ecstasy during orgasm. Making love is a union of souls, and an opportunity for both partners to connect in the deepest and most profound way known to man.

3. The Marathon
Sexual marathons are best when you have a lot of time. Start with lengthy foreplay in bed before moving to the shower, then back to the bedroom to try out a plethora of positions. As

well as time, sexual marathons require privacy, preparation and a big glass of water next to the bed. A weekend away without the children is the perfect time to enjoy a sexual marathon.

4. The Quickie

The 'quickie' is about fast satisfaction. For example, it's late and he wants sex, but you have to get up early. You feel a little in the mood already and know that if you don't have sex now, you'll stay awake for at least another hour saying, 'No, it's too late,' to each other. So what do you do? Rip your clothes off and take action. Just remember, sex is not all about quickies — even if your husband says it is.

Ultimately, your sex life should contain a combination of quickies, marathons, making love sessions and basic sex.

The female orgasm

Some researchers believe that there is only one type of female orgasm, while others suggest there are two types. In more recent times, some researchers have suggested there are three female orgasms. Well, it's no wonder there is such confusion surrounding the female orgasm.

An orgasm is the peak of sexual arousal, when all muscles, that were tightened, relax. You can have an orgasm during sexual intercourse, foreplay or masturbation. During an orgasm, your body may experience any of the following: waves of pleasurable feelings throughout your mind, body, vagina, pelvis and uterus. Your body may tingle, or goose bumps may appear on your skin and your muscles throughout your body spasm (mostly in your vagina, uterus, anus, and pelvic floor). Your heart beat and blood pressure rises, your breathing speeds up and endorphins are released. These endorphins commonly leave you feeling elevated, inebriated, happy, giddy, relaxed, sleepy, flushed, exhilarated and less inhibited.

What is important to remember is that these changes vary greatly, from orgasm to orgasm. One night you may feel like yelling your partners name at the top of your voice, in sheer ecstasy. The next time you have an orgasm, you may think, 'Oh, that was reasonably pleasurable. I feel nice.'

Apparently, one in three women has trouble having an orgasm during sex, particularly a uterine orgasm. Not being able to have an orgasm during sex could relate to any of the following: His penis size could be an issue (maybe the fit is not right), you may be too inhibited, the foreplay, or sex, may not be long enough for an adequate level of arousal, or you may have a low sex drive.

The three main types of female orgasms:

1. The clitoral orgasm (vulval)
Most women experience orgasm through clitoral stimulation, rather than through vaginal penetration. This orgasm is achieved by direct stimulus to the clitoris, usually by you, or your partner's hand, during masturbation or sex. The throbbing sensation during a clitoral orgasm is extremely intense, and is felt mostly in the concentrated areas around the vagina and pelvic regions. Many women are able to have clitoral orgasms during masturbation. Some women are able to have clitoral orgasms during sex, if their partner stimulates the clitoris with his hand, during sexual penetration.

2. The orgasm during sex (uterine)
A uterine orgasm (orgasm during sex) is achieved by the vaginal penetration alone. This orgasm does not produce the same

changes in the body, as a clitoral orgasm. While the clitoral orgasm is concentrated in the vagina and pelvic region alone, the uterine orgasm is more likely to affect the entire body and mind. Some women have described this orgasm as being 'on a pleasure cloud', with waves of intense pleasure rippling throughout the body. Others have described feelings of intense euphoria. Women having this uterine orgasm usually experience a combination of: goose bumps, hot and cold sensations, muscle spasms, and an overall pleasurable sensation through the body and mind.

3. The blended orgasm
The bended orgasm is a combination of both the clitoral orgasm and uterine orgasm. One way to achieve this orgasm is for your partner to stimulate your clitoris during sex.

Not having orgasms?

It is possible that some women are confused about orgasms, and could, in fact, be having orgasms, but not realizing because 'the earth did not move'. Yet, what they could have had was a small orgasm.

If, after sex, you are left feeling sexually frustrated, or if you felt no peak in your sexual arousal, then it's possible that you did not have an orgasm.

Interestingly, women who masturbate apparently have a greater chance of having orgasms. Why? Well, they are more accustomed to pleasuring themselves; they know what to look out for, what works, and what doesn't.

An orgasm during sex involves a great part of the mind. For his reason I have listed below: '10 tips for more orgasms' below.

The Big O — ten tips for more orgasms

Many women rarely, or never, have orgasms during sexual intercourse. Women are such complex creatures and it can seem as though the earth, moon and planets have to line up before having an orgasm is possible. A lot of women think it is their partners fault if they are not having orgasms — think again! A woman's mind and attitude make a huge difference to her ability to have orgasms during sex.

Following are ten simple steps that should help you have more frequent, and more intense, orgasms.

1. *Relax your body*. Keep your body relaxed. Have a massage or shower before having sex.
2. *Clear your mind*. Keep your busy mind still. No thinking about shopping, children or work. Think of nothing except pleasure.
3. *Focus on three things: sound, touch and pleasure*. Think only of the sounds of your partner breathing, his touch and the pleasurable feelings in your body.
4. *No negative thoughts*. Don't let negative thoughts such as, 'Am I too loud?' or 'Can he see my cellulite?', enter your mind.
5. *Release your inhibitions*. Relax; a man loves to hear you moan with satisfaction. Don't be scared to be a little vocal, as it's perfectly natural when floating on waves of pleasure.
6. *Feel the sensations*. Focus on every sensation in your body such as hot, cold, wet, goose bumps and eventually orgasm.
7. *Squeeze the vagina*. For a more intense orgasm, squeeze the pelvic floor muscle during your (or his) climax.

8. *Variation.* Change sexual positions whenever you feel like it. Don't simply lie on your back the whole time and expect to have multiple orgasms. Experiment with positions that work, and then change them, for the best possible chance of multiple orgasms.

9. *Praise your man.* When it feels awesome, tell him. Your praise will give him the confidence to try new ways of pleasing you.

10. *Enjoy.* Whether giving or receiving pleasure, enjoy!

Create a mood

Some women are almost always in the mood for some friction under the sheets, for others, preparation is required. To ensure the best results, try to be well rested and relaxed. Take the children to a babysitter every now and then, or put them to bed early so you and your partner can give each other undivided attention. Try to create a romantic mood in the bedroom, or any other room in the house, by experimenting with music, dim lighting, candles and champagne. Lamps in the bedroom are a necessity, as bright lights during sex are a turn off for most women.

Dirty Talk

Don't be scared to experiment with a little dirty talk. Go outside your comfort zone to experience more pleasure. It is amazing how just uttering a few crude suggestions will get most men in the mood in less than a minute! Try it out. You may be surprised. Tell him what you want to do to him, step by step, and don't leave out any details. Don't be scared to be crude. Men love verbal foreplay. While you may feel a little uncomfortable saying, 'I just want to unzip your pants, kneel down in front of you and suck your c***,' it's bound to appeal to your man. Act it up a little and try to get into the role. Try to use words you wouldn't usually say and resist the urge to laugh.

One friend said that since she had started talking dirty to her partner, she no longer had trouble getting him in the mood for sex. She was excited to have finally found the key to getting more sex. Her only regret was that she didn't start talking dirty to her partner years ago.

Sexy clothing — Lingerie — Kinky Toys

It is essential for every married woman to own an assortment of lingerie, sexy clothing and sex toys. Buy to suit your partner's tastes. Aim to have outfits or accessories, suitable for any occasion or naughty mood. Add some excitement to your love-life by including some of the following pleasure items in your collection.

Clothing, Lingerie, Toys & Accessories

Try and have a couple of nice 'teddies' in his favourite colour and style, corsets (these are expensive but slimming), crotchless panties, garter belt and stockings (a black set and a white set), at least one pair of stay-up stockings, fishnet stockings, knee high boots, tight sexy pants and/or mini skirt.

Rush out and buy some: handcuffs, blindfolds, vibrators, chocolate body paint, whipped cream, baby oil and edible massage oil. Half the fun will be buying them!

Fantasies and Games

It is not wrong or abnormal to have sexual fantasies — everybody has them. As men are more sexual, they tend to have more sexual fantasies than women.

Don't be scared to share your fantasies with your partner. Act them out together. You will go through stages where different things will turn each of you on. During one sexual encounter you may be blindfolding your partner, the next time, he may be handcuffing you to the bed, or you may be painting each other with chocolate body paint or licking whipped cream off each other's bodies.

Exploring your sexual fantasies with each other will take your passion to the next level (as long as you're both comfortable every step of the way). You may be nervous, shy, or laughing the whole time, just make sure the adventure remains fun. Don't participate in fantasies you don't enjoy.

Dress-ups for two

Do your marriage a favour and have fun with dress-ups and role play. Ask your partner to tell you what style of dress-up honestly appeals to him. Try one of these kinky outfits for starters: leather/vinyl pants, short black dress, leather mini skirt, low-cut top, see-through black lace top, nurse's uniform, maid's uniform or schoolgirl's uniform. Imagine, for a minute, that you are a married man with an attractive wife. Wouldn't you want to see your wife dressed up in one of your fantasy outfits? Ask your partner to dress up for you too. You may want him to grab out his old army uniform or wear a suit and tie, to push your sexual buttons. If there is nothing to wear in the cupboard, go out and buy him a cowboy hat or a uniform of some type from the second-hand shop. He is bound to look sexy in a uniform. The idea is to escape from your comfort zone and add more spice to your sex life.

Striptease

To do a great striptease for your partner, hire Demi Moore's *Striptease* (1996) movie on DVD. Practice alone, in front of a full length mirror. When you feel in the mood, tell your spouse you are going to do a striptease for him. Wear an outfit you feel sexy in, that will turn your man on, and wear sexy lingerie underneath. If there are no children home, let the lounge room be your stage. Otherwise, lock the bedroom door for the performance.

Ask hubby to sit down for a strictly 'look but no touch' performance. It is all about the tease and not the nudity. Let's face it, once your clothes are off, the strip tease will be over! (Your man will make sure of that).

Role play is something a little different and can be surprisingly arousing. At the very least, try to do a striptease every few months for him.

Dirty dancing at home

For a great night, on birthdays, anniversaries etc., try some dirty dancing.

Preparation:

- Buy little tea candles to place around the lounge room.
- Choose a CD of romantic music and set up the CD player.
- Have alcohol at the ready.

- Book a dinner for two at your favourite romantic restaurant.
- Buy snacks and hire romantic DVD's to watch later in the night.
- Arrange to have the children babysat for the night.

Action:

Prepare the lounge room as discussed above, then dress up and go out for dinner to a romantic restaurant. As soon as you arrive home light the tea candles, have a drink and put the CD on. Pull your partner in close and start slow dancing. The air will be full of romance as you dance to the heartbeat of your partner, and your favourite songs, in a room full of little candles. If your partner is the type of person who always says no to a dance in public, then this is your chance for a bit of slow dancing. Feel the heat in your body and find no reason why you shouldn't start dirty dancing in the privacy of your home.

Sex Show for one

Irrespective of how painfully shy you are, most men have an inbuilt desire to examine their partner's naked body. The sex industry, including tabletop dancing, strip clubs, topless bars and lap dancing venues, survives because its serves a fundamental purpose: almost every man has an innate need to not just admire the naked female body, but to study it. It's quite simple. All women have the same body parts. We women certainly don't find our genitals — or his for that matter, particularly fascinating to look at. Yet, most men find their partners private regions fascinating to study.

Most men crave little sex shows from their partners, so be

adventurous next time your partner asks you to do something different. Try to be a little less inhibited. Surely you would rather your partner look at your anatomy in wonder, than stare at a stripper's!

A man with erection has altered perception

Men are biologically programmed to focus on their partners positive physical features, and screen out any physical imperfections, while they are having sex. When aroused, men's bodies have an increased level of dopamine, which causes them to view their partner's bodies more favourably. Maybe their second brain is less critical than their first brain. Anyhow, it certainly makes you feel better, doesn't it?

Let your nightie say it all

Rather than him having to ask you for sex all the time, why not let your nightie say it all? Use your nightie to give your husband a clear, unmistakable message. Have three outfits for bed and wear them depending on how you feel. It will certainly take the boredom out of dressing for bed.

Yes nightie: This is your sexiest nightie. Wear this outfit if you are feeling frisky and are definitely in the mood for making love.

Maybe nightie: This nightie is more comfortable, but still a sexy nightie. It is for those nights when you're feeling undecided, but may be able to be persuaded into a little action.

No Nightie: The PJ's or matronly nightie gives a clear, 'I just want to sleep. Leave me alone! Don't even give me that randy look', message to any game pursuers.

Caution: This system doesn't always work as planned. Why? Well, this system was designed by a woman, me, yet men think differently. Men, even the married ones, still love to chase, catch, and then drag their women into the bedroom. As a result you may find you are being chased even more when you wear the 'No Nightie'.

Try the system out for yourself. It's a fun way to change the mood in the bedroom all the time, as you won't have the same look and feel every night. One night you could be wearing cotton, the next flannelette and on the third you could be wearing satin.

Just be careful not to wear your 'no nightie' all the time, regardless of how comfortable it may be.

Middle of the night romps

You really haven't had sex until you've had 'middle of the night sex'. This is truly mind blowing. If you're already having it, then you will understand what everyone is talking about. If you have never tried it, then do yourself a favour and experience it ASAP. The best middle of the night sex is when you both go to bed feeling a little aroused, but you don't have time to have sex. It is late and you have to work tomorrow, so you simply kiss goodnight. As you're sleeping, your bodies take over. You find yourself, or your partner, groping, feeling and teasing, without even being consciously aware of what is happening. You wake up aroused and start having sex with your partner while you are not totally alert. It's as if your body has decided to take control and your mind (at least your conscious mind), has little to do with the experience.

All your senses (taste, smell, sound, touch) are heightened during sleep resulting in the chance of more intense orgasms.

The combination of prolonged foreplay, the ongoing teasing and touching through the night, and your relaxed state of body and mind, can contribute to the most explosive sex ever!

Star in your own video

Many adventurous couples film their own pornographic movies starring themselves and their partners. Try it out and have some fun. Watch your movie together and have a giggle, then tape over it. It is just another fun, sexually courageous, thing to do.

Buy some mirrors for the bedroom

If you don't want to record yourselves, why not place a few mirrors around the bedroom. It can add another level of eroticism to your bedroom activities. You certainly don't have to get a mirror installed on the ceiling above your bed — although it is a fabulous idea. Just place a mirror strategically positioned, on the wall of your bedroom.

* * *

Interview with a sex worker

To further explore the reasons why men pay to have sex, I decided to visit an established, high profile brothel and interview a sex worker. The sex worker agreed to a half hour interview at the same rate as a full service ($115). When I arrived the receptionist introduced me to Kylie. Kylie is in her mid forties, blonde, beautiful, tall and appeared to be size 14 (which surprised me, as I assumed all sex workers were size 10 — silly me). She was outgoing, friendly, mature and certainly did not fit the stereotype I had in mind of a sex worker. She was easy to talk to, professional in every way, empathetic towards her clients and very understanding of their needs. She greeted me wearing nothing but a sexy bra, knickers and a very small see through nightie. Her finger and toe nails were manicured, her make-up was immaculate and she wore extremely high heels, which she kicked off half way through the interview. She made me a cup of tea and proceeded to tell me all about her unusual occupation.

Kylie said: I look after and support my children and parents. I was married years ago, with a beautiful home, but lost most of my money in a bad investment. I have previously worked as a barmaid, along with other jobs. I love sex, so this is the perfect job for me. I don't have a boyfriend — this is my sex life. I get paid for what I enjoy. A lot of girls in this industry are like me. Sure, like all jobs, you have your great days and your night-mare ones. My friends tell me that I shouldn't earn money for sex. I tell them that they have sex for drinks at a bar, so why shouldn't I get paid money for sex? I keep half the money that I make. I have an ABN and it is all legit. I earn from $350 to $850 a week, but then again, I sometimes make $850 in a day. I get paid hundreds of dollars one day and go spend it the next, because I know I can come back the following day and earn more. I do want to find a 'real job', as I am getting older and it will become harder to get work.

How long have you been working in this industry, and what age are your clients?

Five years. 18–96 (clients must be over 18 years old). The average age is between 30–60 years old.

What do most clients usually want?

More tender loving care than anything else. I'm different from most of the other girls; I'm friendly and don't rush them. They are here for a reason. Of course they want sex, but they are looking more for TLC and special attention. You need to be an actress to do this job. Men come in here needing something they are not getting from their partners. So, from the moment I speak to them, until the moment they leave, I act like they are the only man on the planet. They get what they are usually not getting at home . . . a woman's undivided attention.

Do you have many regulars? Do you know if any of your regulars are married?

Eight. They visit weekly. All of them are married.

Do you ever become friends with your regulars?

Yes. They tell me about their lives, their jobs, their partners and their children. They want companionship. They talk about their worries, I give them advice. Sometimes one will arrive in tears and talk about his wife kicking him out. They often want a shoulder to cry on, like a man would talk to a barmaid. Some get attached to me. Some of them want to rescue me. You have to be careful with some regulars, as they can start to think they own you. Some think I'm not 'in here' because I want to be. They don't realize I have a choice. They tell me that they can get me out of this place and set me up, look after me, so that I can become their mistress. I don't want that. They don't understand that I am free now. I would not be free as a paid mistress. I would lose my independence. Some married women think they are free, but they are getting paid to have sex every night in an unhappy marriage.

How many of your clients are married?

About 80% of our clients are married. Single guys do come in, but most are married.

What are the married men coming for?

Like I said earlier, married men come for attention, TLC, cuddles — especially the ones over 60, they in particular want lots of really good cuddles.

How many of your clients ask for head jobs?

Almost every man who walks in the door wants a head job. Most of the men who come here are not getting head jobs from their partners, as the guys usually say, 'My girlfriend (or wife) doesn't do this for me'.

Anal sex?

A man's fantasy and curiosity. I don't do this, but one of the other girls does. Some men just want to know what it's like to have anal sex and their partner doesn't do it. It's not that common a request.

Straight sex?

Yes, we get the 'tradies' coming in for 15 minutes of sex. They are usually stressed out and working hard, and just want a quick release so they can get back to their work and perform better.

Kinky sex (D&B)?

Not many people want it here, at this place, as we have no dungeon.

Role play?

Not common. I've never seen it in my five years. I assume you're talking about the woman dominating the man?

Dress ups?

Yes. I don't do that much, but one of the other girls has a nurse's, school girl's and police woman's uniforms. These requests, believe it or not, are not that common.

Girl on girl?

This is every man's fantasy (and every woman's fantasy if you're honest), so occasionally a guy will pay to either be with two women or watch two women make out.

What about that 'private dancer song' by Tina Turner, where it says 'keep you mind on the money and your eyes on the wall'. Surely, that can't be true. Wouldn't these guys need you to focus on them and connect, by looking them deep in the eyes, etc?

My boss, the owner, is very spiritual. She talks about things on a deep level: these guys are coming here for more than just sex, so we need to give them more than just sex. I focus entirely on them and make them feel special; like they are the only person in my life; like there is no-one else.

What else do they want that their wives don't do? Do they talk about their partners? If so, what do they say?

Head jobs, a woman showing an interest in them, spice. They just say, 'we don't get this at home, now that we're married with children,' type of thing.

Do most of these married men appear to fit into one of the following categories?

a. Have no confidence (low self esteem) that needs building with female attention?

A few.

b. They seem to have a high sex drive and just need sexual release?

Not really. The 'root rat' picks up sex for free. There are plenty of women out there having sex for free. The root rat can't afford to pay us as often as they want sex. Paying for sex doesn't fit their stereotype.

c. They just want to do things different with a professional that their wife will not do with them at home?

Some men come in to learn how to have sex, as they see themselves as failures in the bedroom with their wives. Many of these men seem to have really small dicks and can't satisfy their wives. This is sad, as what wife is going to stay with a man who can't satisfy her?

d. They are normal every day men, who just need sex every now and then, as their wives are not really that interested in sex anymore.

A lot. This is the most common reason. Most of the clients I see are normal guys, who just want sex and attention, and they don't get it from their partners.

Why do men visit a brothel instead of having an affair?

They see it as convenient, no stress, no repercussions and hassle free, over and done with in half an hour and it cannot be traced back to them. Even the credit card bill comes up as a motor parts company.

What are some of the other reasons that men visit brothels?

Some women pay for their husbands to have sex while they are pregnant or just after having a baby. They know the sex worker is clean and it's better than an affair. Some disabled men come to have sex.

How many times do you have sex a day?

I work 10.00 am until 5.00 pm Monday to Friday. I can have sex up to seven times a day. I have not had any clients today (it's about 12.15 pm). Sometimes you just sit around and wait for a job . . . that is hard.

What is the busiest time — nights or days?

The nights, especially from Thursdays, are the busiest. The days are not as busy, but I work during the day as I have children. During the days you tend to get more of the older clients, in their 50's and older. During the nights you tend to get more of the younger guys.

Do you have orgasms with your clients?

Yes, especially the older clients. The only problem is I try to not let myself have too many orgasms, as you don't feel like having sex again that day. So, I usually try and pretend. Most guys know that you are faking, but it's better not to have too many orgasms to keep up your stamina.

As you see so many married men, do you have any advice to give married women?

Too many women seem to think that when they get married and have children that their husbands will stop wanting sex just because they have. This is not true. Nothing changes in his world; he still works, comes home and wants to have sex at night. The only difference is that after having children, many women don't feel like sex anymore. This is when he misses out. Keep the spice in your relationship. Don't let it get mundane. If you're driving along and you both feel randy, stop at a park and have sex in the car. Have nights out alone together. Keep things fresh.

Homework

It's all in the eyes

Next time you make love with your partner, gaze lovingly into their eyes and continue to do so until you both climax.

It is such an intimate and bonding experience and will give your marriage a spiritual lift.

You may be lucky enough to be doing this already, but sadly, not every couple looks intensely into each other's eyes while making love.

* * *

Hot night workout

On the next hot and humid night, spread baby oil all over each other's naked bodies and make love.

You will need lots of towels or old sheets on the bed for this act.

This kinky fantasy needs to be acted out at least once a summer.

How well do you know each other?

Learn more about your partner's sexual preferences.

A. Use two pieces of paper, one for you, and one for your partner.
B. Write the numbers 1–12 down together with your answers to the following.
C. Swap your pages when you have finished and compare answers.

1. Which of your partner's outfits do you find the sexiest?
2. a. Is your husband a more of a 'boobs, bum or a legs' man?
   b. Is your wife more of a 'chest, bicep or butt' woman?
3. Which part of your partner's body do you find the sexiest?
4. Name one thing that is guaranteed to turn your partner on?
5. Are you more attracted to blondes or brunettes?
6. What is your biggest sexual fantasy?
7. What is your favourite part of foreplay?
8. What is your favourite time of the day or night for sex?
9. What is your favourite sexual position?
10. Which other activities arouse you while having sex?
11. How long do you usually spend on foreplay and having sex?
12. What do you usually think about while masturbating?

Step Eight

How to avoid or survive an affair

People having affairs are watering someone else's garden, while neglecting their own. They are not living life fully.

Keep sexual thoughts on your partner

If you're going to fantasize about someone, fantasize about your partner. The mind is one of the most powerful instruments in the universe. Always keep your sexual thoughts about your partner. There is a very important element to making love, or having sex, that is not often talked about, but it is of paramount importance to the ultimate sexual experience. My theory, which I call 'The Mind Equation', is based on a scripture from The Holy Bible. The Holy Bible explains that adultery is committed first in the heart (i.e. mind), then in the body. 'If a married man is to look at a woman (who is not his wife) with lust in his heart, he has already committed adultery in the eyes of the Lord'. (This is not an exact quote.) This powerful scripture has remained burned into my mind for over a decade. It is saying that just to look at someone who is not your partner, and fantasize about having sex with them, is adultery and therefore, a sin. This may seem harsh, but it will keep you out of trouble and do wonders for your sex life with your partner. I will explain how.

The Mind Equation

Acknowledge the attraction to another person (other than your partner), but do not dwell on, or entertain, these lustful thoughts in your mind. Your subconscious mind cannot easily distinguish between imagined (mental rehearsals) and reality (events that actually occurred). Of course you will have a fleeting lustful thought about someone, here and there, that quickly enters and leaves your mind. This is because you are only human after all and find people from your species attractive (not just your partner).

Athletes mentally rehearse winning to help them achieve their goals. Do you want to mentally rehearse being with someone else and thereby risk losing your marriage? Any mental rehearsal (lustful thoughts about someone who is not your partner) is sexual energy directed away from your partner. This does not help your sexual relationship with your spouse, as it will reduce your ability to fully enjoy lovemaking.

Having sex or making love, involves the mind and emotions, not just the body. If a woman is not connecting with her partner in mind and spirit while making love (because she's thinking about someone else), then she has a reduced chance of having an orgasm.

While it is possible to have great sex while lusting after someone else, the chance of having an intimate lovemaking session involving a deep soul connection would be impossible.

Making love is the union of two souls. It is love, expressed in marriage, in the purest form. You couldn't possibly look lovingly into your partners eyes while making love, and climb to the heights of passion, while feeling betrayal, guilt or lack of interest.

The Mind Equation relating to fantasies

Affairs start in one place — the mind. Be careful with your fantasies. Keep your mind on your partner. Most people have sexual fantasies, but it's far more enriching for your marriage to base your fantasies (even during masturbation) around your partner. Doing this will strengthen the bond between you and improve your passionate encounters. Ideally, you and your partner are attracted to each other, lust after each other and satisfy each other. If you think about someone else during masturbation, it cannot benefit your relationship.

When you think of sex, think of your partner exclusively. If you can't do this, try and find ways to improve the attraction between you and your spouse.

5 reasons why people have an affair:

1. Searching for that special feeling again.

The feelings of infatuation (new love) are so wonderful they can make you feel alive, physically and emotionally. Some people, who have moved into a more comfortable loving feeling with their partner, end up seeking this infatuation elsewhere. Craving the feelings of infatuation, they may start flirting innocently with someone other than their partner. Soon they begin to feel infatuated with the new object of their attention. When this occurs you need to stop and evaluate your life, and decide if the direction you are heading in is really where you want to go.

Do you want to end up having a quick fling, which could quite possibly end your marriage, or would you rather put the missing 'oomph' back into your relationship?

2. Are your needs not being met?

The reasons why affairs begin are not complicated. Most adults need friendship, conversation, attention, excitement, intimacy, flirting and fun. If your partner is not meeting your needs, you will often look for someone else who can. It is simply the law of cause and effect.

Sometimes a person may not even be consciously aware their relationship has changed or that they are no longer satisfied. As strange as it seems, we always attract into our lives what we want. If we want more fun and romance with the opposite sex, we may subconsciously attract people into our lives that can give us these things, but that may also lead to an affair.

When you think about it, affairs are just new relationships while one (or both) partners, are still in an existing relationship. Affairs usually begin when the primary relationship changes over time and some needs that were being met at the start of the relationship, are no longer being met.

3. Better sex.

Many people have affairs because they are unsatisfied with their sex lives, not having sex often enough, or not attracted to their partners anymore. Sex is a basic human need, after all. Many men, who love their wives and children, have a girlfriend on the side to have sex with. It is also common for men to go to prostitutes for sexual acts their partners won't perform, most commonly oral sex. Now that's a pretty good reason to be adventurous with hubby.

4. Have you married a bull?

Some men are like bulls and some are like cows. The bull wants to have sex with every cow in the paddock, and the cow is happy with one sexual partner. Now, if you've married a bull, you know all about his huge sex drive. He loves you, but he worships all women. He is a perve and a crazy flirt. While many bulls are happy just to look at other women (and chase their wives around the house every day for sex), other bulls will chase most attractive women they meet.

As bulls tend to have higher sex drives than average men, they usually drive their partners crazy, asking for sex constantly. The good news is a bull's sex drive can eventually decrease over time. If bulls are kept busy and are satisfied in their careers, they are easier to live with as their sex drives diminish. The bull that is unhappy in life, bored with his work, or not having enough sex at home, is more likely to have an affair because his need for sex is so great it can literally consume him. He can easily become obsessed with sex.

Men who play a lot of competition sport usually have a high testosterone level, which makes them more aggressive, more competitive and often raises their sex drives. Many of these men are bulls.

If you have married a bull, keep him entertained and busy with lots of jobs around the house and garden. Hopefully his sex drive will be a little more manageable.

5. The other person makes you feel fantastic.

Do you assume that a man married to a beautiful and attractive woman would never have an affair? If he did, do you assume it would be with a more attractive woman? Think again. Surprisingly enough, most 'other women' are often less attractive than the wives who are being cheated on.

Why would a man have an affair with a less attractive woman? Well, when men have an affair, it's usually *not* just about the sex. One of the most common reasons a man has an affair is because the other woman makes him feel special and gives him lots of attention.

So, it doesn't matter if you are size 8 with the face of a beauty queen, if you're treating your man like a dog, instead of a king — be careful. He may just rush off with the chubby neighbour two doors down, who bakes him cookies and listens to him talk endlessly about his football team.

Your mind can lead you into an affair

Our minds play a large part in creating our destiny. We attract people, places, jobs and events into our lives through our repeated thought patterns. There is much more to our lives than what we see and touch.

Have you ever noticed that when you want something badly enough, an opportunity will just seem to magically appear? For example, if you desperately need a few hundred dollars, you luckily receive an unexpected windfall or your boss asks you to do a little overtime.

This mind power can work for or against you. If you're thinking about anything which could be harmful to your life and relationship (such as having coffee with an ex boyfriend), then be careful because believe it or not, you often actually get what you wish for in life.

Flirting: The two different types

When it boils down to it, everyone flirts. Flirting can be fantastic for your self-esteem, your confidence and your happiness. It can make you feel younger and more attractive. A flirt here or there, with a complete stranger in a safe environment, should be harmless and incident free.

1. Flirting for fun. People in great relationships flirt with their partners regularly. And even if you 'make eyes' at a friendly petrol station attendant every now and then, these small flirtations should do nothing but make you feel attractive. As long as you never divulge personal information and keep your distance, no harm will be done.

2. Flirting for need. It is potentially dangerous when people flirt with others because their needs are not being met in their relationship. As they are not flirting enough with their partners anymore, they need to flirt constantly with others. This can eventually lead to affairs.

Be careful who you flirt with

Try and keep a little distance between yourself and men, other than your husband. If you flirt with your workmates, relatives, in-laws, neighbours, friends or anyone else you see regularly, it can lead to trouble. How many times have you heard the words 'office affair'? People usually don't plan to have an affair with a work colleague. These things take time to develop and usually start with one thing — flirting! Communication often flows endlessly between work mates. Sadly, some people make the mistake of becoming too close, letting their colleague in on too much of their inner world by having intimate conversations all the time. Combine these intimate conversations with flirting and fantasizing, and you have a dangerous cocktail. Also, when you are at work, you are usually showing others your best side, as you are paid to be on your best behaviour. People on their best behaviour can seem flawless. They can put up a front, tell lies and manipulate you, while your sweet partner at home is being his true self.

Flirting is an extremely dangerous form of communication with the opposite sex. Flirt with caution.

Internet affairs

Internet affairs are very common nowadays and have become a problem worldwide. When someone has an internet affair it all seems to start so innocently, and then before they know it, the other person becomes an obsession, an addiction that becomes hard to stop. These relationships start with daily communication using email, instant messenger, chat, ICQ or SMS. Most or all, of their emotional energy is directed towards their internet friend, while they pay little attention to their partner.

Quite often these relationships develop past an emotional affair, whereby the people involved arrange to meet each other and the relationship becomes physical.

People can fool themselves into thinking that they are doing nothing wrong, by rationalizing that they are simply talking to someone on the internet. They cannot see the bigger picture. They become oblivious to the negative changes in their life and often end up neglecting themselves, their children and their partners, due to the time they spend communicating with their internet friend. In most of these online relationships, the internet friend becomes the 'main relationship', while the 'primary relationship' takes a back seat. These relationships are destructive, and ever so sneaky, as they start off so innocently.

Don't panic yet. If you are in a fulfilling relationship with your partner, there should be no need to run and hide the computer keyboard and mouse. A happy partner is not likely to turn into a cyber dater.

After baby affair

Before many women get pregnant for the first time, their husbands are usually their whole universe. They adore them, worship them, cuddle them and have regular sex with them. However, when a woman becomes pregnant, changes start to take place in her relationship with her partner.

A woman changes while she is pregnant. She may withdraw physically and emotionally from her partner. Her priorities change and her partner may not be her top priority anymore. A pregnant woman can often be more demanding and less attentive to her partner. This is nature's way of keeping the mother-to-be rested.

Other changes occur after she gives birth. Mother Nature protects the newborn by making almost every new mum obsessed by the new arrival. For a while after most women give birth, they can think of nothing else but the baby. This love and connection with the newcomer is so strong that it is similar to the infatuation that she initially felt for her partner, but it happens in an instant at the time of birth! While many men are included in the whole pregnancy and birth process, some men feel rejected, left out or jealous. Men need lots of daily attention, and they need to feel wanted and appreciated by their partners. Some women neglect their partners after giving birth, and this neglect can continue for years, in some cases, until their partners feel like an outsider in their own home. Some men are so desperate for female attention again, that they seek it elsewhere. While it seems positively unthinkable, some men start an affair soon after their partner gives birth. This type of affair is just another example of when something is lacking in a relationship, people will seek what they are missing from someone else.

We all need someone to love us and appreciate us. Yet so many women neglect their first love (poor hubby) when their second love (the children) comes along. Don't forget to continue to love and appreciate your partner after the children come along.

Scent based sexual attraction

In most animals, pheromones (odourless chemicals) play a vital role in the mating process. And while not often discussed, these chemicals also play a huge role in sexual attraction, and choosing a mate, in humans.

Have you ever met someone and thought, 'Gee, they really aren't that good looking, but wow, they are so sexy?' This is because sexual attraction is often more about how you 'smell', than how you look. The whole attraction by scent (pheromones) is also a highly selective process; our body 'odours' may be perceived as pleasant to one person, and unpleasant to another.

When it comes to finding a mate, we are more attracted to someone who's genetic based immunity to disease is most different from our own, thus creating a stronger foundation for healthy children. In short, your body is constantly seeking someone with a healthy mix of genes, to best create healthy children with. Your body has no conscience. Accordingly, if you find someone overwhelmingly attractive (and you are single), then at least on a biological level, you have a better chance of creating healthy children together.

On the other hand, if you are married, and you meet someone, other than your spouse, who you find incredibly sexually attractive, run the other way! Every so often you will meet some one who just takes your breath away. It's these extremely strong sexual attractions that you need to be most aware of (if you are already married).

Animal attraction is just that: instinctive and animalistic. It goes beyond just our minds, right through to our primal urges. Many affairs have started from an overwhelming sexual attraction, which over time, becomes a relationship, then an affair. The best way to handle this strong sexual attraction, if you are married, is to avoid the other person.

If you are lucky enough to have this instinctive, primal attraction to your spouse, then that's fantastic. Because even when you are fighting with him, you can still feel like grabbing him and kissing him.

Are you too busy working?

Today's society is very materialistic. Often both partners work to pay the car loan, credit cards, house mortgage and to keep up with the latest commodities. These financial pressures, in addition to the time spent doing everything else (paying bills, doing chores, cooking, shopping and being a taxi driver for the children), places many couples under stress. If they are not careful, husbands and wives end up having little time left for each other.

You don't need a spare partner

While it sounds incredible, some people start affairs then rationalize that the other person is a spare, thus ensuring that they will never be lonely. If the primary relationship does not work, they can fall back on the secondary relationship. This does not make sense. When you need to put all your love, focus and energy into one relationship, you are assured you won't need a spare. Yet, if you're trying to give everything you have to two relationships, you are guaranteed to end up unhappy. You may feel comfort knowing you have a spare partner, but each of your relationships will be incomplete.

Affairs destroy the soul

Not many people who are conducting an affair are truly happy. From speaking to a number of women who have had two men in their lives at the same time, and from my experience of an emotional affair, I can conclude the following: Most affairs end in tears, sooner or later.

The heart, body and soul have space for only one partner at a time. Talk to anyone who is having an affair. Look at the pain and confusion in their life. Look at the deep sadness in their eyes, despite an outwardly happy exterior. Ironically, having two people in your heart will usually make you more lonely, miserable and distraught. Not to mention how life destroying the feelings of guilt can be.

Stopping an affair

If you decide to end an affair, trying to avoid the other person may feel similar to a drug addict who is coming off drugs. Why? Well, when you are infatuated, you are like a drug addict; you can become erratic, unpredictable and highly emotional. The infatuation drugs (endorphins) may take away your ability to think logically. For example, you may take risks that you would normally never consider. So trying to avoid someone you have a crush on, and forcing them out of your mind, is similar to giving up smoking. By severing contact with someone you are infatuated with, you're literally reducing the level of endorphins in your body. Logically, you can reason with yourself that you're doing the right thing, but you will go through a period of grief and withdrawal from the 'love wonder drug', endorphins. (This is possibly why some men find it easier to leave their wives and children, rather than leave their lovers).

What if your partner is having an affair?

What happens if you stumble across a note in your husband's wallet and discover he is having an affair? Obviously you will be angry and need to work through many of your emotions. However, first of all, you need to sit down and analyse your relationship. Do you want to stay with your partner? Is this the end of your marriage? Do you understand why your partner did this? Can you think of any reasons? Is he likely to end the affair?

While it may be hard, try not to neglect him and shut him out emotionally at this time. You will need to work together and seek help. If you shut him out, it will make matters worse. Many marriages can survive, and some even improve, after an affair. There will be a period of mourning for the trust you have lost. Eventually that trust and love can come back, if there is no more adultery.

There are two sides to every affair

While talking to my hairdresser recently, I asked her if she had heard any juicy marriage, or affair, stories. She told me that one day she had two women getting their hair done, at the same time, who were sleeping with the *same* man! One of the women was the wife, the other was the mistress. All of the hair-dressers knew what was going on, but the women didn't. What made this so funny was that it seemed like the two women were talking about different men: The mistress was saying how lovely her boyfriend was, yet the wife was complaining about how horrible her husband was.

I think the message behind this is that a husband will usually treat his mistress better then his wife. So, why not become your husband's mistress, and wife, at the same time?

Avoid affairs by keeping your distance

One of the most painful experiences in life is to 'love' two people at the same time — it is soul destroying! For this reason,

I suggest you only cultivate close friendships with people of the same sex. It is impossible to have emotional affairs, leading to physical affairs, if you don't have close friends of the opposite sex in the first place. While this may sound harsh, life is complicated enough without adding problematic relationships, which could lead to the demise of your marriage.

If you find someone else attractive, acknowledge the attraction to yourself and make sure you don't become really good friends with them. The safest thing you can do is keep a little distance between yourself and the opposite sex.

Emotional affairs (triangles)

What is an emotional affair? An emotional affair involves three people: you, your partner and someone else (a triangle). It usually starts as a friendship that you or your partner has with another person that develops into a deep emotional, rather than a physical connection. (While the relationship is not usually a physical affair, physical attraction is often a key element in emotional affairs).

An emotional affair occurs when a strong friendship is formed between yourself and someone who is not your spouse. It may be with someone you work with or met online. It could be your neighbour, brother-in-law, or best friend's husband.

The key factor in emotional affairs is the regular conversations, which are usually conducted daily, by phone, face to face or over the internet or mobile. When you are having an emotional affair, you prefer talking to, flirting with and spending time with the other person, while you often neglect your own partner.

An emotional affair can be just as devastating as a physical affair. However, emotional affairs are deceptive; they sneak up on the participants and leave marriages in ruins. Often the people involved don't even realise what is going on until it is too late.

While most emotional affairs are with people of the opposite sex, you can also have an emotional affair with someone of the same sex. In some cases, a close friend of the same sex, or even a mother-in-law, can end up being the third person in the triangle.

Of course, you need to have relationships with friends and family, just make sure that you and your partner are the team. Your partner should be the person you turn to for most of your daily chats. Have an affair with your husband. It is fulfilling, convenient, guilt free and should last a lifetime.

* * *

A triangle involving a third person should never exist in a marriage. I know this from first hand experience. A decade ago an emotional affair almost destroyed my marriage.

Two years after we were married, we had our first child. During this time my partner and I drifted apart and were fighting continually. I had just started working in a covers band, as a singer, and was close friends with my female and male band mates. I developed a crush on one of my male band mates. I would chat with him almost every day, either at rehearsals, or on the phone, yet tragically, I would merely wave at my partner when he walked in the door after work.

Over many months my marriage deteriorated because I was spending almost all of my emotional energy on my band mate and hardly any on my partner. I became increasingly unhappy. I could feel that something was not right in my relationship and my life, but I felt like I was in a hole and couldn't get out.

What made things worse was that my partner was standing

back, waiting to see if I would have an affair or not (he told me this later). He had withdrawn emotionally, so that if I left him, he would not be hurt as deeply.

My infatuation became stronger, and I felt so much guilt. I knew my crush was wrong. I had to make some big decisions quickly, if I were to save my marriage. I thought it would help my marriage (and ease some of my guilt), if I told my partner of my crush, so that's what I did. I needed to cut all ties with my band mate if I hoped to keep my marriage. I told my band mate that I was so sorry, but I would never be able to speak to him or see him again. It was painfully hard, but looking back it was the only decision to make.

Strangely enough, the whole experience brought my husband and I closer. I vowed never to get into that situation again by making a conscious decision that I would put back into our fractured relationship what was missing. I realized even then, that for the crush to have developed there must have been many problems and an emotional disconnection between my partner and I.

It was after this painful experience that I created the steps in this book so I could restore the friendship, romance and passion in our marriage. I wanted to have a crush on my partner, not anyone else, and I wanted this crush to last forever. With these steps, I have succeeded so far.

Do you actually love the other person?

When I had a crush on my band mate, I sat down and tried to analyze how I felt about him. I wrote a list of all his good and bad points, and my partner's good and bad points. I then realized that what I loved about my band mate was the way he made me feel! I loved the special way he treated me and how

I felt when talking to him. When I stopped to think it over, I realized he was not even my type of person at all. All the characteristics that I really loved about my partner, my band mate did not even possess. Standing back from my crush, I could see clearly that I wasn't in love with my band mate; I was in love with the way he treated me.

* * *

Inside the mind of a mistress

Susan, who I spoke to recently about her long affair with a married man, lives two separate lives. The real life (she is a housewife, goes to work and takes the children to sport on the weekends), and the escape life (she meets her lover for hot passionate sex in hotel rooms or in her own home). Susan has been having a secret affair for more than three years. She confessed that she rarely does anything for herself, apart from the affair. I asked Susan many questions in an attempt to understand why she continued to risk her marriage over this fling.

She said the sex was amazing and she found the whole experience with her lover thrilling. She said her husband was useless and boring in bed, and he was not interested in foreplay. He had also gained weight since they were married and she was not that attracted to him anymore. Susan claimed her affair was only about the sex. She said she did not love her lover, but actually loved her husband.

What amazed me about Susan was that she was a typical working mother. Her appearance was conservative. She certainly did not fit the stereotype I had imagined of the type of woman who cheats on her husband. She told me that she risked everything because the sex was so amazing, however, I don't think that many women would risk breaking up their family, just for great sex. I felt the real reason was deeper than that.

Her escapades came from the heart of a martyr; a woman who did everything for everyone else, and this affair was the only thing she did for herself.

I believed she was infatuated with her lover, but denied her true feelings to herself. She seemed bored with her husband, her work, and her life, except for the affair. This affair appeared to be her escape from the monotony of her life, as bizarre as that sounds.

Some people actually have an affair out of boredom. Someone who is passionate about a variety of interests, or their employment, and has plenty of friends, is less likely to have an affair.

Interview with a bull (player)

My objective for this interview was to find out why some men cannot remain faithful to their partners. Is it because they have a higher than normal sex drive and one partner cannot satisfy their sexual requirements? Or is there a deeper psychological reason that stops them from being faithful?

Paul is in his late twenties, highly intelligent, a great conversationalist and incredibly handsome. It was easy to see, in an instant, why women (and men) throw themselves at him constantly. He is successful in his work and fantastic with money. To most women he would appear to be the perfect catch, however, he has one problem: he usually dates two or three girlfriends at a time. Paul confessed that he currently has two girlfriends; one he has been seeing for a year and the other for a few months. He says that he loves only one of his girl-friends and finds his most recent girlfriend annoying at times.

What sort of relationship do your parents have? Have you ever felt abandoned by a parent?

My parents have been happily married for over thirty years. My dad always let me quit. I would get all ready for a new sport, then tell him that I had changed my mind and he would just drive me home. He was never consistent. Also, my parents moved homes every couple of years while I was growing up. I had to make new friends every time we moved.

Have you ever had your heart broken?

Yes. She was hot, sexy and looked like a model. She would do anything for me and loved sex. She ended up being unfaithful, but she denied it. We were dating for six weeks then she broke my heart.

Have you ever been faithful?

Yes. I once went out with a girl for two years and didn't cheat on her. She was marriage material. She came from a good family.

What percentage of your relationships would you be faithful?

About ten percent. Most of my girlfriends have been an 'eight week f***'. It takes that long to figure out if we both want the same things in life. I am constantly looking for a wife.

Do you love the thrill of living dangerously? Do you crave variety and need to have more than one girlfriend at a time?

Yes, I love the thrill. Yes, if a person is not right, I'll need more than one girlfriend.

Do women throw themselves at you? If so, does this make being faithful hard?

Yes. A lot of unattractive women, and also men, throw themselves at me.

Where do you meet your new girlfriends? Work, nightclubs or other?

I hate nightclubs. I mostly meet new women by being introduced to them by friends. Sometimes I meet them through work, but I don't like to put my dick where my money is.

How often do you see and speak with your girlfriends? Isn't it hard keeping track of conversations?

I see them both about three times a week. I also talk to them every day. I call them both the same pet name, so it's not confusing, but it is hard at times.

Why do you find it hard to remain faithful?

I usually find fault with them. It usually boils down to their direction in life. I'm scared of getting married and finding that I'm stuck with someone I'm not compatible with.

Do you feel like you hold back emotionally from your girl-friends?

I give everything to my girlfriends. I don't hold back. But on the other hand, if a girlfriend tells me that she wants to leave, I just point to the door and tell her to get out, as it's over. I don't change my mind and I don't fight for the relationship. There is always another girlfriend. It's like, 'next!'.

Are you happy with the quality of the sex with your girl-friends? Do you think you are addicted to sex? Do you think you have a higher than normal sex drive?

Yes. Yes. Yes.

How often do you want to have sex?

Daily, but I can easily do it a few times a day. Once I slept with three different women in one day.

How often do you have sex?

About five times a week.

What do you think a normal sex drive is?

Once or twice a week.

Do you crave attention or just need lots of sex?

It's not about attention at all. I just need lots of sex.

How many women have you had sex with?

About one hundred. I meet them, date them and then discover that they are not what I am looking for, so we split up.

Have you ever paid for sex?

My mates shouted me a prostitute at a brothel once, but I walked into the room and just couldn't do it. I had more fun watching my mate have sex with her. That was a good laugh.

Do you feel any guilt? If so, what do you tell yourself?

Yes. I tell myself that it wouldn't have worked anyway. I'm not totally happy with any of my current girlfriends.

Do you try to be faithful, but your urge to have sex is just too high?

Everyone can control themselves. If you're driving home from work and you're hungry, that doesn't mean you have to stop the car and have take-away. Your sex drive is the same. You can wait until you get home.

Do you love the mating game (the excitement of dating someone new) so much that you keep looking for a new partner?

I have to weigh up the time-cost factor for all relationships. I need to budget that into my decisions about new relationships.

Do you get bored easily in relationships and life?

Yes, life can be pretty boring. T.V. is boring.

What type of woman would make you be faithful?

A woman who is sexy and looks like a model. She needs to be mentally stimulating as well and not weak (like my girlfriend).

Do you look forward to settling down with one woman?

Yes, but I can't see it happening.

Do you think your high sex drive and frequent unfaithfulness are genetic, and you are unable to change?

No. We all have self will. Mmm, genetic? I had never thought of it that way before. I wonder?

Do you honestly think that the human species is meant to have only one mate?

I think the idea is beautiful.

* * *

Are you having an emotional affair?

- Is there someone who you think of as being like a brother or sister?

- Do you wish you could get on as well with your partner as you do with the other person?

- Do you have more fun with other person, than with your partner?

- When you are spending time with your partner, do you wish you were spending time with the other person instead?

- Have you drifted apart from your partner?

- Do you feel more sexually attracted to the other person than your partner?

- Do you feel confused about your marriage?

- Are you unhappy with your marriage?

- Do you feel happier when you are spending time with the other person?

- Do you feel like the other person understands, and listens to you, more than your partner?

- Does the other person treat you better than your partner?

If you mostly answered yes to these questions, thank goodness you have this book. Help is only a few pages away.

Are you heading for an affair?

Does your partner fulfil your needs? If he doesn't, then you could find yourself heading for an emotional separation, resulting in an affair. Does your partner:

- Flirt with you and tease you lovingly?
- Make you feel wanted and special?
- Listen to all your thoughts and plans about life?
- Lust after you and make you feel sexy?
- Hug you daily?
- Make love with you often?
- Have passionate sex with you often?
- Cheer you up when you are feeling down?
- Take you to fun places?
- Share your dreams?
- Keep you grounded when you feel unstable?
- Put your needs before his needs?

If you answered yes 10–12 times: You have nothing to worry about. Your marriage appears to be in excellent shape. You seem very fulfilled by your partner.

If you answered yes 7–9 times: You seem very satisfied with your relationship, but may have a few issues. For the most part, your relationship seems excellent.

If you answered yes 4–6 times: You seem to be struggling with a few issues and possibly not feeling satisfied with the quality of your relationship.

If you answered yes 0–3 times: You seem to need serious help. You may have drifted apart over time, and either of you may already be having an affair.

Is your partner having an affair?

If you suspect that your partner may be having an affair, look out for the following warning signs:

- He starts putting more effort into his grooming routine.
- He starts dieting.
- He starts a new fitness routine to tone up or lose weight.
- He starts working late or working irregular hours.
- He buys new clothes.
- He goes out more frequently by himself.
- He buys new aftershave.
- He buys himself new underwear.
- He starts getting text messages/emails and views his messages privately.
- He spends a lot of time on chat websites, forums etc.
- He becomes increasingly distant.
- He starts to criticize you more often, to reduce his guilt.
- He has sex with you less frequently.
- The sex you are having is different than it has been in the past.
- He starts cleaning the car more often (inside and out).

If many of these warning signs happen simultaneously — panic!

Step Nine

Children should enhance, not destroy, your marriage

Most couples find that having children completes them. These little miracles enrich and transform our lives on a daily basis, in a most magnificent way.

Childbirth changes a woman forever

When a woman gives birth to a child, it is a life changing experience. Due to her greatly increased responsibilities, she quite often neglects her husband for a little while after the big event. It is important that a man understands that on some level, his wife has been affected and fundamentally changed by the birth, more so than him. This can cause jealousy; especially if his wife is ignoring him and devoting all her attention to the little newcomer.

Childbirth is like a little hurricane

While your life may change after having children, it is still possible to enjoy loads of romance with your partner after the children come along. If you continue to spend time together every day and follow the steps in this book, the romance in your relationship should not diminish.

Some couples almost expect that their relationship will deteriorate after having children, but it doesn't have to. In contrast, having children gives you the opportunity to deepen your love and commitment.

Creating balance in your life

Once women have children, they often become less focused on themselves, their work and the rest of the family, if only for a short time. And while their children demand a large part of their time and energy, new mothers need to remember to keep their life balanced. Once they have settled in with the new baby, they need to work at sharing their time fairly between their children, husbands and themselves.

Teach your children about life

They may be children now, but you are actually creating the adults of the future. Do you want your children to grow up to be hard working and responsible adults? Do you want your children to love to work and play, just as much as you do?

By contributing to the household chores, just as they would be expected to if they were an employee or a flatmate, they can get a sense of teamwork. When I was growing up, I would always help in the kitchen, with the shopping, and do my own laundry. If your children grow up with their parents doing everything for them, they will always expect someone else to clean up after them.

If you give your children everything on a silver platter and ask for nothing in return, they will think life is just like that: all take and no give.

Praise your children daily

Children need constant praise. It is vitally important! It is right up there next to 'love them and hug them'. If you tell your children with all sincerity how wonderful they are, how great they are at school, how neat they are, how good looking they are and how clever they are, they are more likely to excel in many areas of life.

When parents stop praising their children for their good points, this is usually when the children start developing bad attitudes or falling behind at school. Next time any of your children starts developing a bad attitude, ask yourself, 'Have I been praising them enough lately? Have I been giving them enough quality time lately?'

You are continually contributing to their sense of self worth. If you show constant love, support and praise, you will give your children the confidence they need to pursue their dreams.

When I was a chubby little girl in primary school, my mother would tell me I was beautiful. I was freckly faced, with frizzy, curly hair. When I had a bad day at primary school and was being kicked in the shins by my only friend, my Mum would comfort me by saying, 'You are beautiful. All the other girls at school are just jealous'. Even in secondary school, when nasty girls would start fights with me, my Mum would say, 'They're just jealous of your beauty'. Even though I didn't really believe her, her praise made my world so much easier. Her praise made me feel secure and emotionally supported in a world that was unkind. At the very least, I felt at peace when I was at home. Without her constant praise, love and support, it would have seemed at times, as if my whole world was ending. I think her continual praise is one of the reasons I have the confidence and belief that I can do anything I set my mind to.

You don't know what is happening in every minute of your child's life. Children live in a world full of fear, control and vulnerability. They need your praise, love and support to make it through the tough times.

Never argue in front of children

Try to think of children as sponges: everything they see becomes a part of them and affects how they behave now and as adults. Children also interpret things very differently to adults. When children watch their parents argue, they're more likely to think that they are going to divorce. They don't understand the complexity of marriage and that disagreements are bound to occur. More than anything, children need to feel safe in their world (without constant hostility, yelling and violence).

For your children's sake, try to argue when they are not watching. Or if they are old enough, explain that everyone argues. It is a part of life and you still love each other.

Circle of life

Before we got married we went to see our local priest, Father Peter, for the marriage preparation class. He gave us some golden advice, which I would like to share with you. Father Peter told us that when a couple are engaged and become married, they are at their closest so far. Then as a couple goes through life, and the children start coming along and life gets busy with all that comes with parenthood, the relationship changes. During these family years, some marriages remain strong because both husband and wife remain focused on each other. Sadly, some husbands and wives drift apart from each other during this time, as their focus shifts from each other to the children, work commitments and everything else that happens in life. One of two things can happen when the children eventually grow up and leave the nest:

a. You and your partner rejoice in the love you still have. You cherish the time you now have to spend together. It is literally a full circle. You are both alone together again; able to enjoy each other, just like when you first got married.

or

b. You and your partner realise that you have drifted apart from one another, with all the responsibilities of parenthood and the fast pace of life. You realise that you have focused so much energy on either the children or your separate careers, that you are strangers, simply sharing a house. You realise you don't feel connected, and haven't felt connected to each other in years, so you divorce.

How do you want to feel about your partner when the children leave home? Don't neglect each other for the sake of the children and all your other commitments. The children will leave one day, and you and your partner will be the only ones left sharing the house.

The circle of life that Father Peter mentioned to us is:

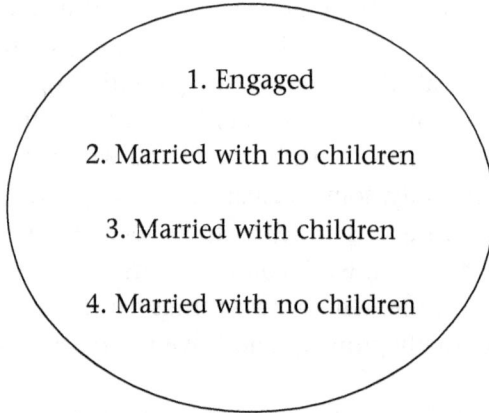

1. Engaged

2. Married with no children

3. Married with children

4. Married with no children

If you keep the connection during the busy years, you will have a stronger chance of keeping the connection right through until you grow old together.

You cannot put your relationship on hold until the children grow up. Your children only live with you for part of your journey. Your partner hopefully lives with you for life.

Homework

Have a weekly children's night

Make your children feel totally spoilt, cherished and adored by having one night per week dedicated to doing fun things with them.

A weekly children's night is fantastic for your relationship with your little people.

We started this night, which we call 'Special Friday Night', when my first son was six years old. Every Friday night, we go down to the supermarket and he picks out one bag of chips, a chocolate bar and some lollies. We also hire a movie to watch at home.

We started this tradition for a couple of reasons. Firstly, I felt my son and I weren't getting enough quality time with each other. Secondly, to my horror, most of the children in Prep at school were eating chips, chocolate and lollies every day for play lunch and lunch, while my son was having an apple and a vegemite sandwich. So I started having our Special Friday Nights and my son eats junk food once a week.

Special Friday Night has been going for over eight years, and it's a family tradition that even the adults enjoy.

Step Ten

Argue effectively

An argument is an opportunity to understand what is going on in the mind of your spouse. Once the argument is over, consider the issues that need to be discussed to avoid further conflicts.

Don't be scared to argue

Fighting is perfectly normal. It is the frequency of the arguments, the way couples choose to argue and the resolution of the arguments, that determines the difference between a happy or unhappy marriage.

Three 'Golden Argument rules'

By following these three golden rules and the ten tips for resolving conflict, you should be able to decrease your time spent arguing and increase the productivity of your arguments.

1. Never go to sleep on an argument

Avoid going to sleep before an argument is resolved, at all costs. Even if you have to stay awake talking until 3.00 am. This is far healthier than trying to sleep after participating in an unresolved argument with your partner. Going to bed before settling an argument is one of the best ways to keep anger inflamed, and is guaranteed to make arguments last longer.

When you sleep your subconscious mind is busily sorting out and filing all your thoughts and emotions from the day. The subconscious mind doesn't simply file your thoughts; it expands and plays with many of them first. If you have just had an argument, the hurtful thoughts of anger and pain may be acted out in dreams while you sleep, and this could happen most of the night!

It is no surprise if you wake up feeling like you want to punch your partner after going to sleep while in the middle of an argument. You have most likely been fighting with him in various dream scenarios, while you were sleeping.

2. Never sleep in separate beds

My Grandmother once told me to never sleep in separate beds after an argument with my partner. As she was happily married for more than 50 years, I considered her advice to be sound. If you sleep in the same bed, you have a far greater chance of resolving the argument. You may even start to regret nasty words, as you look at your partner sleeping away like a gentle giant. If you have been emotionally wounded, and feel like a cuddle, you can just reach over and hug your partner. (Now that's a great argument stopper!)

Sleeping in separate beds just keeps any argument or hostility alive. It is not the way to stay happily married.

3. Never have long silent treatments

When some couples fight they resort to the silent treatment, where one or both partners stop talking to each other. While this can be a very natural reaction after a fight, helping you calm down and think, silent treatments that last more than a day are harmful. It is far better to confront each other and talk about the problem, than it is to ignore each other. If something you are doing could harm the relationship, like giving your partner the silent treatment, it should be avoided.

Silent treatments may be fantastic for most men, who probably enjoy a bit of peace and quiet while their wives are not talking. However, if you're anything like me, trying to keep silent and hold everything inside for a long period of time, is enough to cause an emotional volcanic eruption.

Silent treatments make it easy for resentment to build, as issues are not being discussed and problems are not being resolved. Silent treatments are best avoided, or at the very least, kept short and sweet.

When did the fighting begin?

If you have been disagreeing, on and off for many months, try to think back to when the bickering started. In every struggling marriage there was usually a point when things started to deteriorate. Pinpointing the reason for the negative change in your relationship enables you to make the changes necessary to improve the situation.

For many couples an increase in their financial burden, moving house or changing jobs, strains their relationship. Many couples are fighting because their lives are over committed; leaving little time for each other.

You are far better off resigning from a weekend job (if the weekend job is the problem), than getting a divorce.

Resentment destroys marriages

It is really important to avoid letting resentment build towards your partner. Long-term anger has negative consequences, not only in your marriage, but also in your life. If there is a matter that needs discussing, do this as soon as possible so issues can be resolved quickly. A problem shared is often a problem solved. A problem buried will often lead to resentment.

If your partner makes you angry, feel the initial anger briefly, then deal with it. Don't let it destroy your peace. Try to either confront him or forgive him, so that your anger dies down. Anger and resentment are negative energies, which will usually bring negative outcomes into your life. If you are living with anger towards someone, you cannot have total peace in your life. It is harder for you to love life, yourself and others, while filled with resentment.

Resentment can also lead to illness. Author Louise L Hay, talks about how our mind and emotions affect our bodies and lives in her brilliant book, *The Power Is Within You.* She explains in great depth how to change your thought patterns to improve your life. If you eliminate as much anger from your life as possible, you will have a greater chance of having a better marriage.

Resentment destroys marriages as it blocks the flow of communication, spiritual connection and love between husband and wife.

Ten quick tips for resolving conflict

1. Identify the problem then try to find a solution

a. Identify the problem: Whose needs are not being met in the relationship? What are the issues behind the argument?

b. Find a solution: Discuss possible solutions with your partner when he calms down. Often people simply need to express their feelings in order to feel a lot better. Make sure you both have the chance to explain how you feel. Just being heard is often enough to improve the situation.

2. See life from your partner's perspective

If your partner comes home and bites your head off when you're simply asking what he wants for dinner, ask yourself why? Is he worried about your financial situation? Is he going for a promotion? Is he unhappy at his place of work? Has he just spent the past hour in peak hour traffic, with no air conditioner?

Understanding the reason for his anger does not excuse his harsh treatment of you, but it might give you a glimpse inside his life. Imagine walking in his shoes to try and understand his actions.

By looking at the situation from a different perspective

should keep you from dragging out any arguments longer than necessary.

3. Swallow your pride and compromise

Love and hate are such powerful emotions; the person you love one minute can easily feel like a person you could hate the next. Let's face it, being the person who stops an argument is difficult, but it is usually worth putting your pride on the line to get back to peace and love again. So swallow your pride and stop arguing. Compromise can make you happy, fast. Of course, you may not feel like making up and would rather throw a tantrum, but a relationship is all about give and take. Stop the war. Peace is far easier to live with.

4. Life is short, so argue quickly

How would you feel if your partner died in a car crash today and your last words to him were nasty? Never let your loved one leave your side without a kiss. The worst thing to do when you are arguing is to keep the dispute going for days. It is best to sort things out as quickly as possible.

It may help to have some time away from the children, and any other distractions, to sort through the issues and resolve the disagreement.

Letting an argument drag on for days is terribly destructive. It will make you unhappy in your relationship and in your life. Life is too short to be unhappily fighting with our loved ones. Fighting is such a waste of energy.

No one is guaranteed tomorrow. Our time on earth with our loved ones is limited. Enjoy them. Don't spend all your energy arguing with them. In any moment you are either improving your relationship, or ruining it.

5. Avoid friends who criticize your partner

It is important to avoid friends who side with you and alienate your partner, especially when you are arguing. Everyone has opinions, but some friends and family members may really 'fire you up', which further inflames arguments. It's great to talk to a friend about your partner occasionally, and as long as your friend just listens, this should cause no harm to your marriage.

However, sometimes a friend's opinion can add to all the negativity that surrounds an argument. Avoid friends who criticize your partner, at all costs, as it creates more distance between you and your partner in a potentially volatile time.

6. Bring out the old photographs

You may not be feeling deep love when you are arguing constantly with your partner, but it remains buried in your heart. Try to bring the love to the surface by going down memory lane. At times when you are fighting constantly with your partner, bring out some old photographs depicting happier times. The flame is always ready to be rekindled, even after something as soul destroying as an affair.

Looking at old photographs and seeing the deep, underlying love you have for each other, should help bring back some intimacy.

7. Write down the reasons you fell in love

Think back to all the special qualities that first attracted you to your partner and write them down. Writing down all the reasons why you first fell in love with your partner will allow your loving feelings towards him to surface. These longstanding positive feelings should be stronger than your current feeling of anger.

8. The 'ten things I love about you' exercise

To feel close to your partner once again, try the '10 things I love about you' exercise. This is a powerful exercise. Please complete the following steps with your partner:

1. Sit down on your couch.
2. Hold hands.
3. Look deeply into each other's eyes.
4. Taking turns, tell each other ten things that you love about each other.

You should experience a great deal of love and intimacy during this exercise. Just for starters, you may not have held hands with your partner for a long time. In addition, to look into each other's eyes and talk about what you love about each other, is a magical way to strengthen your soul connection.

This exercise, when done correctly, will help bring relationships back from the pain of constant fighting, towards peace and love.

Note: Sometimes it helps to have someone oversee the exercise to make sure that you both stay focused, loving and honest with each other. They can help to ensure that it doesn't turn into a negative, bitching session.

9. A cuddle can make a big difference

It doesn't seem natural to ask for a cuddle from your partner when you are fighting. Yet if you stop to think about it, quite often you actually want a cuddle. Either of you may be feeling neglected, be craving affection, or have unresolved sexual tension (one reason why 'make up sex' after an argument is so popular). If you are able to ask for, or initiate a cuddle, the argument could quickly dissolve, making way for love and passion once again.

It's far easier to explain your side of the argument while you are sitting calmly in his lap, than by yelling your opinion from the kitchen (while slamming the kitchen cupboards).

It's amazing how hard it is to be angry with your partner while you are in their warm embrace. Arguments end faster and more peacefully with a cuddle.

10. Spend quality time together after a fight

An argument can chip away at the core of your relationship, so after making up you will need some quality time together, to repair the damage. This will help to eradicate residual anger and restore your relationship.

If you can't afford to have a night away from the children, at least go to bed early and spend quality time with each other, talking, making love and restoring your friendship.

My favourite tip: keep yourself happy

A great technique in an argument, or tense situation with your partner, is to distance yourself while you both cool down. Make yourself happy by doing things that you enjoy. For example, what would you do right now if you were on a weekend away with your friends? Read magazines, get your toes painted, eat chocolate, have a drink, go for a bike ride? Well, create this frame of mind. Have a bath, go see a friend for coffee, go clothes shopping or watch a movie. You are not giving your partner the silent treatment, instead you are completely switching off thoughts about arguing, as you go into 'please yourself and make yourself happy' mode, creating a bit of space between the two of you while you both cool down.

As long as you are not angry, while keeping your distance briefly, this should not be harmful. It is just like putting the argument on hold for a short space of time. Hopefully, your partner will have time to think and see that you are not storming around in a huff, but instead simply pleasing yourself. He may come to you to resolve the issue, or forget about arguing all together.

Don't be 'shitty' or 'bitchy', even if your partner has said nasty things. Make yourself happy, while giving him the space to calm down.

This is my favourite argument tip, it works for me every time! This should help you both to resolve the issue in a calmer, more positive way. Try it and see what you think.

Don't sweep your problems under a rug

Every time you have a fight with your partner and then make up again, it is an indication that there are issues that need to be discussed. Yet these issues are often left behind once the argument is over. Some couples sweep their problems under the carpet, only to bring them up later causing more arguments.

Don't let your house become a war zone

When you have been fighting for months, or even years, arguments can turn into protests. For example, he may stop mowing the lawns or cleaning up around the yard. You may have a silent war going on between the two of you, causing your home to look more like a battlefield, than a home.

The best thing you can do is to take action. You will feel better, have more peace and less resentment towards your partner, if you do something to improve the situation.

Messy home, messy mind, messy life

If your life is out of control, you will usually have a messy and confused mind. If you have a messy mind, you will normally have a messy home. The more mess around you, the messier your mind becomes, and the messier your mind, the messier your surroundings will be. This pattern continues in an unbroken circle, until your whole life is in a complete mess.

So, if the grass starts getting long and hubby is busy working, mow it yourself or pay to have it mowed. If your house stays tidy, you and everyone in your family, should be that little bit happier and your marriage should be that little bit better.

An out of control relationship does not have to mean an out of control house and garden. If you can maintain some sort of control over your house and garden, you will be more equipped to gain control over your relationship.

* * *

Terrie was unhappily married. Her husband didn't help her around the house or yard. She would pick up rubbish, such as old car tyres, dead branches, broken toys, bits of wood, spare house tiles, and drag it all to the far corner of her backyard. Eventually she had a huge pile of junk in her backyard like a small rubbish tip. She was worried the rubbish pile was harbouring deadly spiders. She was so petrified her two toddlers would be bitten, she wouldn't let them play in the backyard. I suggested that if her husband wouldn't remove the rubbish, that she pay a rubbish removal company to take it away. Even though Terrie could not afford to pay a rubbish removal company to take it away, she juggled the bills and hired them anyway. By taking action her resentment was instantly reduced, improving her life and relationship.

You really have to prioritize when it comes to your family's safety. When you stop asking for help, life becomes harder.

* * *

Homework

Do a R & P Check list

When you have been fighting a lot, you can feel as if you're no longer compatible with your partner. If you feel that it's just not worth it, and would rather give up, do a R & P Check list. This will enable you to evaluate your relationship and see your partner, and your relationship, in a different light.

Grab a pad and create two columns, one called 'good points' and one called 'bad points'. Then write all your partner's good points in one column, and all his bad points in the other. Now, all you need to do is go though the list and put a P or R next to each of the good and bad points.

P is for person. (This cannot usually be changed).
R is for relationship. (This usually can be changed).

Sample:

Good Points		Bad Points	
Intelligent	P	Doesn't flirt with me	R
Hard working	P	Doesn't listen to me	R
Faithful	P	Doesn't kiss me enough	R
		Not affectionate enough	R

If your list looks anything like the above, you have nothing to worry about; all the bad points are relationship issues. These can be corrected and improved, over time.

Step Eleven

Improve your financial situation

Money problems place added stress and pressure on a marriage. When you have a limited cash flow, you have less freedom in your life.

Free yourself of debt

Our whole society seems to buy on credit, then pay back the debt. To get ahead, you need to change your attitude towards debt. You will need to free yourself from debt and start saving.

Make a list of all the debt you have. Any debt, apart from a mortgage, is going to slow down your ability to save. The first thing you need to do is start paying off credit cards, car loans, store cards, or any other debts that you have. If you can restructure the mortgage to pay out the credit card and car loans, this may be a good start (just make sure you cut up the credit cards if you can't trust yourself). Do a budget to find our how much money you need to live on as a family, compared to how much income you are earning. Either you or your partner may need to take on an extra part-time job to earn enough money to cover your living expenses, with a little left over to reduce debts.

Once you have no debt, this extra money can go towards savings for life's little emergencies and spending.

Save then buy

After struggling financially for the first ten years of my married life, I know how not having enough money can affect your relationship in a negative way. Then about six years ago, I read two books that completely changed my financial situation and attitude towards money. The books by author Margaret Bertling, are *Money Maker* and *The Budget Club*. These books simply explain how to have more money in your life and less debt. Margaret Bertling has also written another book, more recently, called *Debt Buster*. You can use the strategies in the books to eliminate your debt, so that the money you earn each week can be yours. You need to gradually pay off your debts (even if it takes a couple of years) and get into the habit of saving. You will discover: it is not always about how much money you are making, but how you spend your money.

Money is not the root of all evil

Life is hard when you don't have enough money to live. When my first son was a toddler we had little spare money due to high debts, including a huge tax debt. My son mostly wore clothes his grandmother bought for him, as we could not afford to clothe him ourselves. Spending $20 on his clothes, when I was thousands of dollars in debt wasn't an option. Needless to say, he wore a lot of old tracksuit tops and pants. I could not be fussy at the time as I was just happy that he had any clothes to wear at all. He had a second hand cot and mattress. My partner and I had the same furniture for the entire ten years we spent in our first home. We could not afford to go out for dinner to restaurants or take holidays, so we didn't.

I feel fortunate nowadays to be able to afford a better lifestyle for us all.

Bills are a part of life

Try not to stress out about your bills. Life is too short. When I open the mail and see a bill, I simply put it in the 'bills' folder. Then on the last day of the month, I open the folder and make a list of all the bills and the amounts owing. I add down the list to a final total. I transfer money around my accounts so that I have enough to pay the bills via internet banking. If there is not enough money in my general account,

I borrow from my spare account. This money is usually repaid over the next week or so.

Everyone has different ways of paying their bills. I'm not saying my way is the best, I just find it the least time consuming and by far the least stressful.

Some couples I have spoken with pay their bills weekly, by using a pre-organised direct debit system. This ensures that they know exactly how much money they have left to spend per week. You can organize this type of payment with your gas, electricity and phone companies. Paying the mortgage weekly is also practical and reduces your repayment time. By paying your bills (and mortgage or rent) weekly, you may find it easier to budget, as the temptation to over spend is reduced.

Teach your children about money

It is your role as parents to instil great money sense in your child, starting when they are young. Children are going to cost you money, whether you buy them toys or you give them pocket money and they buy the toys, so put your children on the payroll! Do you have too much housework? Then pay your children to do it.

My son gets paid pocket money for taking the rubbish out, setting the table, helping with the dishes, making his bed, keeping his bedroom tidy and feeding the pets. We pay him once a month, as a direct transfer into his bank account. His card is always in my wallet, so if he wants to buy anything while we're out shopping, he simply uses his money.

No matter what age you are, it's great to appreciate how wonderful money is, how quickly it can be saved and how much fun it is to spend some of your savings.

Money is made in the mind first

If you change the way you think about money, your finances will change. It works exactly the same as your attitude towards life. If you think like a rich person, then you will be rich. If you think you will always struggle, then you WILL always struggle.

* * *

When I first met Ben and Lisa, many years ago, I was overwhelmed by their very obvious display of wealth. They were business associates of my husband, and we were invited to their home for dinner. When we arrived we walked past the Jaguar and Mercedes, down the steps and past the in ground pool, into the huge kitchen, which over looked the lake, which was right in front of their house. You could just see their yacht from their balcony.

Because we were financially struggling at the time, I felt as if I had walked into a movie. It all seemed so surreal. We sat and chatted in the formal lounge, surrounded by expensive antiques, having alcoholic drinks which were embarrassingly expensive.

It was easy to assume that Lisa had married Ben when he was very wealthy. However, that was far from the situation. I learnt something very important that night: Lisa admitted that when she first met Ben, fourteen years earlier, he did not have a dollar to his name. Ben had always been a hard worker, but Lisa had used her money skills to give the couple the financial freedom they enjoy today. Through her support, encouragement and them both working hard, the couple are millionaires today.

This lesson has always remained in my heart. In some cases, it can take the organizational skills of a woman to bring out the best in a man. When husbands and wives work together, as a team, they can often prosper.

Homework

Start saving 10% of all you earn

- This is the golden savings rule. Every time you or your partner earns money, you need to put aside 10% of this total income.

- This will become a pile of cash that will help to make you feel rich.

- Let this cash pile build, then if you want to buy anything, take the money from this 10% account.

- Make sure that you leave enough money in this account to cover an emergency — don't spend it all at once.

- This will become your spending account for holidays, Christmas presents, furniture or a car.

- Patience really pays off when it comes to saving money.

Once you have savings in this 10% account you will always feel rich.

Step Twelve

Avoid or survive everything else life throws at you

When you get married, you assume it's just you and your partner. But soon you realize there are lots of people, and situations, which you will need to run from.

Avoid living in the wrong house

It is vital to live in a place where you feel happy. It is not possible to feel secure anywhere in the world, if you don't even feel secure in your own home. Your home is your haven, an escape from the world. It is the place where you can recharge your batteries and enjoy time alone or with your loved ones.

Your marriage is greatly influenced by the home you live in. So bear in mind, your marriage can only be wonderful, when you feel wonderful in your home.

When we first got married my husband and I built our dream home, which we loved for many years. However, ten years later, I started to hate living in our ten square house. We had outgrown it and it frustrated me on a daily basis. Our house did not suit us as a couple or as a family anymore. I had lost my sense of peace in that house. I could not go outside and have a conversation with my partner without feeling like any one of our neighbours, from either side, could hear us.

The decision to move was the best decision we had made for years. We quickly found a nice, larger house, in the same area. As soon as we walked into the new house, it felt like home, and we were lucky enough to be able to buy it. Our marriage, and our lives, improved unbelievably when we moved into our new house.

Only live in a house for as long as you want to. Once you feel you have outgrown your home, or it is causing you and your family stress, move as soon as you can afford to. Similarly, if you have spent a long time in conflict with your partner, then moving home to make a new start is an excellent idea.

Just like finding the perfect partner, finding the perfect home starts in your mind. Write down everything you and your partner are looking for in your next home. Have a clear picture in your mind of what you want, then follow your gut instinct from there. It certainly saves time.

When we purchased the last two homes we only looked at three houses before buying each of them. We knew exactly what we were looking for.

Avoid clingy friends

Many years ago, I had a best friend who would stay at my house for hours and hours. She was a lovely person and I really enjoyed her company, but when my partner came home from work, she would not leave. She was constantly overstaying her welcome. She was great fun and we would go to my gigs together, but when I got home I wanted to spend time with my partner.

My partner and I drifted apart during that time as I was too naive to realise this friend was harming my marriage. Every day I gave most of my emotional energy to my friend. My partner was not happy about the situation, but what could he do? It is up to the person who has the clingy friend to do something about the problem and save the marriage.

Marriage is comprised of two people: a husband and a wife. You also have responsibilities towards your children and your family. Continually putting your relationship with a friend before your partner and children will eventually cause marriage problems. It creates a lack of balance in your life.

Do you have a friend who is taking up all your time and emotional energy? This sort of friend will call you daily and want to talk with you all the time, including on weekends. What is left for you to give to your partner? For the sake of your marriage, it's vital to avoid having a friend who takes over your life.

Survive angry outbursts and tantrums

If your partner slams the car door, slams the cupboards, or throws the remote control across the lounge room, take comfort in knowing that most men have temper tantrums. His temper tantrums are just his way of letting off steam. Men are more likely to handle stress by throwing things around, whereas women are more likely to handle stress by yelling.

Yes it is unsettling to all mild mannered females when hubby starts throwing a tantrum, but it is a common way for men to handle stress. Due to their higher levels of testosterone, they handle stress very differently to women.

We level-headed women don't start throwing saucepans around the kitchen, if the spaghetti sauce is cooked, but the pasta is not ready! We save our tantrums for the bigger things in life, like hubby forgetting to tape our favourite T.V. program, like Desperate Housewives.

One time my partner was trying to fix the window in my car door. When he couldn't wind the window up, he became angry and slammed the car door so hard the window broke, shattering into hundreds of pieces. While not funny at the time, we laughed and laughed about it the next day.

Recently I was speaking to a newly married lady, who was rather concerned by her husband's tantrums. I explained that many men have violent outbursts, where they swear or throw things, that it's just their way of letting off steam. It is harmless, providing they never hurt their wives or children. I suggested when it happens in future, that she remove herself (and her children) from the area where her man is letting of steam until he calms down.

Men have naturally short fuses. They are easily angered, yet just as easily calmed down.

Avoid violence in your marriage

It is not acceptable behaviour if your partner is violent towards you or your children. You do not need to tolerate it. A person who is violent should seek help and counselling. There are anger management groups and counsellors which can assist. Contact your local council for further information on the groups available in your area.

Violent people have many similar characteristics, some of which are listed below. Do any of these statements sum up your partner or your relationship?

- Is your partner extremely jealous, controlling or manipulative?
- Does he threaten you, physically or emotionally?
- Does he cry when he doesn't get his way?
- Does he threaten to kill himself?
- Does he act as if you are his whole world and he couldn't possibly live without you?
- Is your partner emotionally unbalanced suffering from extreme mood swings?
- Is your partner extremely immature?
- Has he ever raped you?
- Does he force you to do things against your will?
- Are you scared of what he will do to you if you leave him?
- Have you ever feared for your life, while with him?
- Do you fear he will stalk you if you leave?
- Do you feel trapped?
- Do you feel obligated to him, like you owe him something?
- Does he refuse to talk to your friends or family?

If your partner is violent you have one of two choices:

a. In some cases where violence is an issue, your partner can seek professional help and eventually find better ways to deal with his anger.
b. In other cases, your partner will become progressively worse over time and will become an even greater danger to you and your children.

A person living in an abusive relationship lives with the constant fear of verbal threats, manipulation and violence. The wife and children of a violent man may be threatened, manipulated, physically abused, consoled, rewarded and sweet-talked, but then the cycle can begin all over again.

If your partner has become violent, seek professional help quickly.

* * *

Interview with a survivor of violence

Sandra was beautiful, with dark brown eyes, a huge heart and an outgoing personality. She seemed like a strong woman, yet I sensed she had a painful past. I had a feeling Sandra had something important to say. She told me about her violent marriage.

Well, I felt like I was watching a horror movie as I listened to her. (Some things she told me were too disturbing to include in this book). And while her life was sad and terrifying, she was lucky enough to escape.

Sandra was with her second husband for five years. He was sexy, rugged and the relationship was exciting in the beginning. Yet, in as little as six months, the violence started. She was thrown against walls, punched, slapped, dragged around by the hair, bitten, tied up, had a knife held to her neck, a gun to her head and she was repeatedly raped. Some of her injuries included: broken fingers (from being purposefully stepped on) a burst eardrum, and a jaw that is out of alignment (from being hit across the face so often).

Sandra was not only physically abused, she was verbally abused and threatened. After her husband would belt her, he would say things like, 'Why do you make me hit you? You're so stupid. You know I'm going to hit you when you do that!' He would tell her, 'You're so ugly. Who would want to f*** you?' He would threaten her, 'The next time I pull the trigger, there will be a bullet with your name on it. Your family will think you've run off. No-one will find your body.'

Sandra's husband would get insanely jealous if she talked to anyone while walking across the road to the supermarket. He would slap her across the face when she walked back in the door and say, 'Who was that you were talking to? Who were you arranging to screw?' He would sometimes spit on her and tell her, 'The only good thing about you is my spit.'

I asked the following questions in an attempt to understand why a woman would stay in a situation like that.

Why on earth did you stay with him?

Fear. I believed he would kill me if I left.

Did you really think that he was going to kill you?

Yes. When he put the gun to my head and pulled the trigger, I wet my pants with terror. I did not realize that there was no bullet in the gun.

How could you live like that? How could you cope, knowing that at any moment you could be bashed again?

I used to think about putting dog food or poison in his food, but was scared of what would happen if he found out. I had friends who said they knew people who could break his legs or kill him for me, but I couldn't do that. I kept thinking that my love would change him, so I just kept trying to love and support him.

How did you eventually free yourself of him?

One night he grabbed me around the throat and lifted me up. We were outside in his shed. I really thought I was going to die. My hands were searching for anything I could grab. I could not see. Luckily my hands stumbled on a screwdriver, so I hit him over the head with it. I had never fought back before, but somehow, all of a sudden my fight to survive took over. I felt such strength, like I had never felt before. He had blood pouring out of his head, and he was yelling at me, 'You bitch. You made me bleed.' That was when I changed. It was like a light bulb went off inside me. I told him that if he ever hit me again, I would kill him. That was the last time he ever hit me. He still threw me against that wall, but he would only threaten. He would only hold his fist up and say, 'You're not worth it.'

Why do you think women stay with violent men?

I know that once I got strong and regained my self respect, the bashings stopped. Violent men only bash weak women. You never hear of strong women being abused.

Why do you think your ex husband bashed you?

Well, he was bashed by his father. He had been in and out of jail, and he had hardly any self respect. If he could keep me down here, then he could feel better about himself.

Did he ever apologize?

He ended up having a stroke and years later when I visited him, he said in slow, stuttered, words, 'I hurt you. I'm sorry. This is my pay-back, isn't it?' That was the last time I saw him. He has had a good dose of Karma. He is in a wheelchair and cannot do anything for himself. The hospital came out to measure my house for the ramps. I said, 'What? Do you think I'm going to look after him? We are not together. That man bashed me for five years. 'Do you think I want to spend the rest of my life looking after him?'.

Do you have any advice for women in a similar situation?

Yes. Don't tolerate violence in your marriage. Stand up for yourself. I'm not saying this is an excuse for committing murder, but you do need to take your life back. Positive thinking helps. After I left my husband I focused on the following helpful slogan every day: 'You alone are enough; so believe in yourself.' I am a different person today. I am stronger, happier and finally have peace.

Survive the wedding

Maybe things were different in my day (I was married in 1991), because we only spent $800 on our wedding! We did everything as cheaply as possible, yet our wedding day was absolutely perfect.

My attitude was the wedding would be over in one day, so why spend a fortune? We had built a new home just before we got married and all our hard earned money was being spent on furniture and finishing the house. Our honeymoon was only four days long, but we were happy. We had just spent months building our new home and because we had not yet lived together, we were more excited about moving into our home, than going on a honeymoon. We just couldn't get back quick enough. I couldn't wait to open up all the wedding presents and organize our new little home.

Nowadays couples spend incredible amounts of money on their weddings. Yet an expensive wedding does not guarantee a long and happy marriage. All the weddings I've been to, or performed at (with my covers band), were beautiful, whether they cost $2,000 or $60,000.

I feel sad when I see brides put so much emphasis on the wedding day and so little emphasis on the marriage. Sadly, many marriages fall apart before the couple have even finished paying off the wedding.

Survive the first year of marriage

The first year of marriage (or living together), is a little daunting as your relationship goes through its largest transformation, so far. You are changing from boyfriend and girlfriend, to two people living together, sharing responsibilities and household chores.

Some of the sparkle may seem to disappear from your relationship, because you are now sharing your space more often and your partner is more familiar. It will feel a little strange, adjusting to your partner's idiosyncrasies (like leaving the toilet seat up or never closing the bedside drawers). There are also many other new adjustments to make.

My advice is to lay down the ground rules before any bad habits develop. You can't expect your new partner to be perfect, but think about the types of behaviour which you could not possibly tolerate and tell your partner what these behaviours are, right from the start!

I told my partner I can handle just about anything, but under no circumstances do I want to find clothes or towels on the bathroom floor. The fact that I stressed this point early on in our marriage, is probably why my husband hardly ever drops his clothes on the bathroom floor!

Survive a midlife crisis

I spend a lot of time laughing with friends about the midlife crisis, but it is really a very serious and common occurrence. What is a midlife crisis? Well, if you want the non-technical explanation, here it is: a midlife crisis is when a large change occurs to a person, most commonly during their forties or fifties. It can happen earlier or later in life.

During this phase, the person going through the midlife crisis may change dramatically in any number of ways. They may change their appearance (by dying their hair or joining a gym). They will often change careers, buy a sports car or expensive motor bike, or leave their long-term relationship.

There have been many jokes about the guy going through a midlife crisis who dumps his wife of twenty years, and drives off with his 25-year-old secretary in his new red sports car.

Depression and negative thoughts are also often associated with a midlife crisis. It is often a challenging time for the person going through the change and their family.

Support your partner, as he will hopefully support you, through this challenging time. After all, we should all follow our hearts through life, whether we are going through a mid life crisis, or not. If you or your partner feel like doing something completely out of character (and you can afford it), then go for it. If your partner wants to buy a boat, or an expensive car, or a motorbike, try to find a way to help him achieve his goals.

My partner finally bought his boat and he is much happier and more satisfied with his life.

Survive workaholics

I was talking to a friend the other day who said, 'I don't want to be married to a workaholic'. I said, 'Neither do I. But we are both married to workaholics, so we need to accept it'.

My partner is very much a workaholic. He has Friday and Saturday nights off, a couple of hours on Sundays and a weekend off, here and there, to go away with the family. Any other time, you can expect to find him working on something or other, whether it is a business project, gardening or restoring his boat.

Early in our marriage, his workaholic ways would drive me crazy. I would sit alone in bed at night waiting angrily for him to stop working. I would feel so disappointed, as I was always focusing on the way I thought he should be, rather than accepting him as he is.

Nowadays, I hardly ever get annoyed about him working so much. I am happy with him, because I accept him. We all need to do what makes us happy, even if it is working most of the time. If you are married to a workaholic, try to accept him.

Survive working together

Working with your partner in a business is not for everyone. I have worked with my partner for the past six years in our business and this works well for us. His passion has become my passion and we are fulfilling our dream.

Yet, when my husband was helping me with the covers band, as our sound technician, we fought like cat and dog. We could never agree on anything. It was all wrong. We had so many clashes, that in the end, I found it easier to work without him.

So when people say they are about to start working with their partner, I tell them it could be a nightmare. They need to be prepared to get out quickly, to save their marriage. Alternatively, it may be like heaven, because you can both share the same passion, which adds another dimension to your marriage. Working together in the same business, or even renovating your house together, can put a lot of added pressure on your marriage.

Don't be scared to work together, but be warned: if it does not work, get out while you can!

Survive PMT

Some women I have spoken to have never had pre-menstrual tension (PMT), others have almost lost their marriages over it. One of the worst things about PMT is that when women have it, they often don't realize they have it. They can become irrational, and often lose insight into their behaviour. Women suffering from PMT often feel confused, teary, irritable, nasty, bitchy, highly emotional, unreasonable and frustrated. They often lack concentration and may slip into a temporary depression, if only for a day or two. The physical side affects can include tender breasts and headaches.

I suffered with severe PMT for about a year until my hubby said, 'Why don't you see someone about it? There are drugs for hormonal stuff like that.' I knew I had to do something about it when my mother started diarizing my cycles so she would be prepared for my complete change in personality when PMT struck.

Well, I went to a naturopath, who was also a dietician, and after four or five months, PMT was no longer an issue in my life. My naturopath told me to do the following to reduce PMT: Exercise frequently, reduce or avoid caffeine, avoid highly refined and processed foods, avoid fried foods, avoid foods high in sugar, and eat plenty of wholegrain, fruit and vegetables and raw nuts, such as almonds and cashews. I also started taking B6 daily, which helped a great deal.

For your sake and the sake of your marriage, if you have PMT, seek help. If you are unsure, ask your partner if he thinks you have a complete change in personality once a month.

Survive depression

Depression is a terrible thing and can have a devastating impact on your life, your relationships, your work and your marriage, especially if it lasts a long time.

I am not a doctor, so I cannot speak from a medical point of view, however, I can speak from personal experience. I had depression in the year following the births of each of my two sons. Based on my experience with depression, and from knowing people who suffer from depression, I believe that in many cases, depression is caused when your life is turning out to be different from what you expected or wanted. If many situations, experiences, relationships and life events seem to be out of your control, you may feel like you are the passenger in your life, rather than the driver.

When you are depressed it becomes hard to understand what is going on in your life, you lose objectivity, you feel hopeless and all you want to do is sleep and escape from the world. Everything just seems too hard.

Depression (the mindset)

Open up your mind and really get in touch with your inner voice and your inner needs again. Find your purpose in life. In order to understand your needs, answer the following questions honestly:

- Are you doing what you want to do with your life?
- Do you have good relationships with friends, family and workmates?
- Are you usually critical of yourself?
- Do you tend to judge yourself too harshly?
- Do you go out and socialize?
- Do you have hobbies and interests?
- Do you work at a job you really love?
- Do you put up with people and circumstances that do not make you feel good?
- Do you feel jealous of other people?
- Do you allow other people to criticize you without speaking up for yourself?
- Do you suppress your anger and become quiet, instead of expressing your thoughts?
- Do you feel that life is just too hard?
- Do you have a sense of excitement about your life?
- Do you feel as if life has turned grey?

Depression (get your life back)

Once you have honestly answered the above questions, you should have a clearer picture of what is going on inside your mind.

The next thing to do is to take control of your feelings and your life. Change direction. Move away from negativity towards a positive and fulfilling life. You deserve it!

Once you expand your mind and really think about your wildest dreams and goals, your mind will stay expanded, forevermore with these wonderful ideas.

Ask yourself the following questions to help establish your inner needs, desires and goals in life. Grab a pad and write your honest answers down:

- What do you love doing in life?
- What did you love to do in life before you felt depressed?
- If you were a millionaire, how would you spend your time every day?
- What would you do if you had confidence in yourself and your abilities, both personally and professionally?
- Are there hobbies or activities that you have always wanted to do?
- What are your passions, deep inside your heart?
- Does your inner voice call out with positive suggestions for your life, which you choose to ignore?

Stop saying to yourself that you are not good enough, not slim enough, or not smart enough. These are just excuses holding you back from what would otherwise make you a happy and fulfilled person. Do it! You can change your life, it all starts with living and acting on your thoughts, plans and dreams.

Depression often arises from denying yourself the opportunity to live your life to the fullest. You know you are capable of so much more than what you are currently achieving. You have to start asking for and going after what you want out of your life!

Survive jealousy in the marriage

After much discussion about marital jealousy, it appears there are only two types of people:

a. Those that are insanely jealous.
b. Those that rarely become jealous.

Many people marry someone completely their opposite, so a wife may be insanely jealous most of the time, whereas her husband may not be, or visa versa. If you are a jealous person, it is often much easier to avoid or anticipate the situations which may trigger your jealousy. Similarly, if you are married to a jealous person, then it is your responsibility to be aware of your partner's jealousy issues and avoid making him feel insecure or jealous (within reason of course).

Extreme jealousy forces some people to try to control their partners. How ridiculous! You should never be manipulated by your partner because of their jealousy issues, but you do need to consider their insecurities and possibly make some allowances for them.

I also have a theory that extreme jealousy and a high sex drive often go hand in hand. For instance, most people who appear insanely jealous usually also have a high sex drive. Therefore, jealousy may be an instinctive and primal characteristic.

Jealousy is just another characteristic that you or your partner possess, that allowances need to be made for. If you can accept this aspect of yourself or your partner and work with it, hopefully the issue will not cause restrictions to your relationship.

Jealousy will not magically disappear, but the more secure a person feels in their relationship, the less chance there is that they will feel jealous.

Survive the mother-in-law

All the women I have spoken to feel either irritated or blessed by their mother-in-laws. From these conversations, I believe there are two types of mother-in-laws — the good ones and the bad ones.

Mother-in-laws can be of great benefit to a marriage by giving advice, helping around the house, babysitting and being a great friend to you both. However, in some cases your husband's mother can have a detrimental impact on your marriage. The bond between most mothers and their sons is very deep. She has been there for him through his ups and downs. She was his carer, companion and friend, who encouraged, inspired, listened to and loved him. Then along came you: the girlfriend. He started spending more time with you and less with his mum. Over time, you will take over the roles of carer, companion and friend. You will be the person who encourages, inspires and listens to him. Your husband's mother is obviously still a large part of your husband's (and your) life, but perhaps not on a daily basis.

It is a sad reality for parents, but children do grow up and move on with their lives. Some mother-in-laws cannot cut the apron strings and let go of their sons, or visa versa. Perhaps your mother-in-law's partner has died, or she is not in a loving, fulfilling marriage and may be lonely. In any of these situations, your partner may spend more time with his mother and less time with you. He may not be aware of the negative impact this can have on your marriage. Your partner is turning to someone else daily, but this special role in your partner's life should be yours. This situation is not really different from your partner having an emotional affair. The only difference is that it appears perfectly OK because it is his mother.

When you walk down the aisle you want your husband to be yours, body and soul.

Survive gaining weight

Are you over thirty and having trouble losing weight? I'm certainly no dietician, but almost everyone I have spoken to has said they had no trouble losing weight in their twenties, yet have constantly struggled to lose weight after that. And while everyone understands the importance of regular exercise, diet and smaller food portions, if you are very overweight, you also need to take a close look at your lifestyle.

Often people are overweight because of unfulfilled passions, guilt, anger and resentment, their unhappiness with life or depression. They may be overweight due to lack of motivation, stress or financial hardship. It is a common reaction to overeat, or eat the wrong foods, when you feel stressed or emotional. People who are happy with their lives and relationships, do not generally carry a large amount of excess weight. So if you are overweight, try to face your issues and sort your emotions out, so that you seek comfort from the fridge less often. Once you are ready to commit to losing weight, exercising regularly is often the key. Dieting doesn't always mean eating less food, just eating the correct foods.

Weight loss can be a wonderful boost to your marriage and your sex life. If you have a weight problem, I recommend that you visit a dietician. These specialists can work with you to improve your overall health, and if you need to loose weight, it should be easier with their guidance and advice. Everybody is different. I like most women, have been on every diet known to man. I am much happier, healthier, and can think more clearly, since I started seeing a dietician.

If you are a few kilos overweight and your partner is not concerned about it, then why stress? As long as your excess weight is not a health concern, spend your time worrying about the more important things in life. We are a different body shape in our 30's, than we were as teenagers. If we spend our entire life trying to be the same weight as a seventeen year old, then we will become frustrated.

Don't get obsessed; just eat healthy food when you are hungry.

Survive your nightmares and dreams

Many people take no notice of their dreams and nightmares. Yet, it's in your best interest to analyse them, as they are insightful, fascinating and sometimes shocking. To understand what your dreams mean, is to have an insight into your deepest feelings and a different perspective on your life's events.

Dreams or nightmares are usually one of two things:

a. An important message from your higher self (your subconscious mind), demanding your attention.
b. A thought you had during the day which your mind has expanded or played with, and transformed into a short movie.

During a nightmare, adrenalin caused by fear or shock, is usually released into your bloodstream. This is your body's way of waking you up, so that you pay attention to the important message behind the nightmare.

Your dream or nightmare can leave your mind shortly after waking, so write them down quickly as soon as you wake. If you are keen, keep a dream diary close to your bed, so that you can record and later analyse your dreams.

Dreams are mostly about symbols. Symbols are the most effective way the mind can relay important messages to you. To analyse your dreams you need to decode the symbols and heed the messages. For example, if you dream that you had an affair and totally enjoyed it, then maybe you are lacking romance in your relationship. You would need to address that emptiness quickly. If you dreamt about a spider, and you were terrified, then your body may be attempting to alert you to something in your life which is potentially terrifying, but which you may not have consciously realized. Of course, if you saw a spider the day before the dream, the dream would have most likely just been about a spider.

In our busy lives, we often don't listen to our own hearts (and our subconscious minds), nearly enough. Our dreams and nightmares paint a clear picture of some of our underlying desires and fears.

Survive marrying a clone of your parent

You normally marry someone who has similar characteristics or habits as one of your parents. It's amazing how many women 'marry their dads', so to speak. My father is a conservative, easy going, workaholic, who will only talk 'your leg off' if he knows you. My husband is exactly the same. It's also interesting to see how many men 'marry their mums'. (Maybe this is why so many women find their relationship with their mother-in-law to be such a challenging one. Many women may be very similar to their mother-in-laws).

I had always thought my mother-in-law was nothing like me. I wanted to be a superstar singer, while she was a loving mother and housewife with a huge heart, who loved lunching with friends. Yet, over time I think I have turned into her! The only difference is I help run a family business with my husband. Oh, no! She did the bookwork for her husband's carpentry business. My husband *has* married his Mum!

Survive a break up

Before writing this book, I was a firm believer that the ideal scenario was for all couples to stay together forever. However, after witnessing a couple of separations, I now believe that we all have our own destiny.

Life is a journey, and we travel the road with our partner for a portion of our life, or for the remainder of our life. Some people are destined to have more than one partner, while others have only one.

While I remain a romantic at heart and passionate about saving as many marriages as I can (I believe most marriages can be saved), I still think there comes a point in some relationships when ending the union is best for all concerned. If you find regardless of how hard you try, you just cannot stay in the relationship, you need to accept that as your destiny. Understandably, separation is devastating and can be like mourning a death. But if you have tried all the steps in this book, and explored other options such as counselling, and your marriage does not succeed, remember this: at the end of the day you, and only you, can make yourself happy. It is best to have an independent attitude; you were born alone into this world and you will die alone, so it is important for you to be true to yourself. You will experience some miserable periods as you work through the loss of your partner, but you should try to accept that separating may be your destiny. The overwhelming feeling of loss should not last forever.

Once you start to feel complete again, you can begin to focus on a new life for yourself. Believe in yourself. Be positive that the future will hold many more exciting adventures for you. It is these possibilities you should be focusing on, not the past. You cannot see the future. You could be just about to meet your most perfect partner at the local shops tomorrow. Many people have found love and are totally happy the second or even third time around. Who knows what the future holds for you? If you have a positive attitude and stay true to yourself, the break up may turn out to be the best thing that has ever happened to you. Look ahead to a bright, happy future. It takes time and grieving to heal a heart, but the sun will come out again. And when it does, we can eventually feel whole and happy once more.

Sit down and imagine the type of life, job and relationship that you would like. Plan and envisage the future you want, in order to head in that direction. Sitting around thinking about past failed relationships will not steer your future to the treasures that you so richly deserve. Thinking positive thoughts of a happy path for yourself will help you through the heartbreak.

Survive finding the perfect man

The mind has amazing power. If you ever want something desperately, just focus on that goal. Have faith that you will achieve your objective. Concentrate on exactly the type of person you want, and then let the universe guide you to him.

Soul mates always seem to be able to find each other. When I was only seventeen-years-old, I made a list of all the characteristics I wanted in a boyfriend, and then I met my current partner. He had everything on my list. Was it luck? Or was it because I conjured up the perfect man for myself in my head? Finding the perfect partner starts in the mind

Survive family

Family are fantastic. They make the best of friends and support you through life. But when you get married it's best to keep in mind that you're creating a new family unit. Be careful that your family doesn't harm your relationship with your partner. This can happen in one of two ways:

a. If any of your family criticizes your partner.
b. If you spend more time with your family than your partner.

* * *

Bianca's story: Bianca's father did not approve of her partner (as they were an Italian family and Bianca's husband was Australian). Every morning Bianca's father would come around for coffee and a chat while her husband was not home. Her father would criticize and put down her new husband to the extent that she started to feel a strain on her relationship with her partner. Her marriage was almost at breaking point when Bianca finally realised what was happening.

She took a step back from her father, stopped having coffee with him everyday, and started turning to her husband for lengthy daily chats instead. Luckily that was all she needed to do. Her marriage is still going strong many years later.

Many newlyweds find that their families criticize their partners. Discuss this with your family and do not tolerate it. If this fails, then you will have no alternative but to spend less time with your family, to avoid a negative impact on your marriage.

Homework

Don't give up on love, just because you think it is easier

It is not enough to just love, support, and care for your partner. You need to worship, flirt and romantically connect with him as well.

Many people believe it is easier to leave a relationship, than to fix a relationship. Most people have one of the following mindsets:

Mindset A: Marriage is forever. If we run into problems, we will work at the relationship and find a way to bring the marriage back to love and romance.

Mindset B: Marriage is a journey in life with another person. If it's not working out, then move on and start a relationship with the next person.

There is no right or wrong.

It
depends on
what works for you
the way you were brought up
your expectations and opinions
about marriage
your religion
and
what is in your heart.

About the Author

Why did I write this book?

Over a decade ago, three years into my marriage, our relationship was almost over and I blamed myself for almost destroying it. I had fallen for another man — someone I worked with. I had been living in an emotionally barren marriage, with a very distant husband. I felt like my life was over as I had broken my husband's heart. My heart was broken too. That was the last of many mistakes I had already made in my marriage. I was determined to make my marriage passionate, full and loving.

Why had my marriage gone so far off the tracks in only three years? Well, I had broken the marriage rules. Yet, I didn't know what the rules for staying happily married were! When I got married everyone said. 'You have to work at marriage.' But I didn't know what that meant.

When my marriage was at its worst, I sat down with my tears, regret and depression, and made a commitment to change my marriage. I needed to make rules for myself, rules that happily married couples already followed, and use this strategy to not only be happily married again, but to stay that way.

The marriage rules I created are the basis for the steps in this book. I have followed these rules for the past decade of my married life and I feel closer to my husband with every passing year. I can't imagine being in a more perfect marriage, or being more in love with him than I am today. Naturally, I am passionate about helping others who are struggling with their marriages.

These rules have completely turned my own failing marriage into a passionate and loving union again. They have also enriched the marriages of many couples since.

Are you a naive newlywed?

When I first got married, I was so naive. I thought relationships were this simple: people date, fall in love, become engaged, marry and the fairytale love stays the same forever. I wasn't prepared for the challenges of complicated life events, which throw perfect marriages off balance.

No one taught me how to be married. The good news is that I have since learnt:

a.   You can salvage and improve your relationship any-time you feel it is worth the effort (it is definitely worth the effort).

b.   You can stay blissfully happy, year after year, just like honeymooners.

Who am I?

I am not a doctor, psychologist or professional counsellor. I am a wife and mother (probably just like you). My husband and I started dating twenty one years ago. We have been married for sixteen years and have two children.

What is my training?

Life. This book is based on my own experiences in marriage, and on the feelings and experiences of many women I have spoken to while researching and writing this book for the past three years.

What would I know about marriage?

I know the deep pain and suffering that comes from an empty marriage and I know the envy I had for friends in their happy marriages. Most importantly of all, I learnt how to turn my marriage completely around back to a loving union, and keep it that way for over a decade using these steps. It is possible to turn almost any unhappily married couple back into honeymooners.

What did I do?

When my marriage was almost over, I sat down and thought deeply about my relationship and my partner. I realized my husband was everything I wanted in a man, but he did not treat me the way that I wanted him to. In just about every way we were having trouble in our relationship, but I did not know why. I wrote a list of what I wanted from my marriage and then based on positive thinking concepts, common sense, and my experience and from studying happily married couples, I made a short list of steps for myself to restore my marriage. These steps are the entire basis for the twelve steps in this book.

What did I want from my marriage?

- I wanted to be totally fulfilled in my relationship.
- I wanted my husband to be my best friend and talk with him daily about our lives.
- I wanted to spend special quality time with him every week, enjoying each other.
- I needed to feel like we were heading in the same direction in our lives (or at least know and understand each others' direction).
- I wanted him to flirt with me, desire me and give me lots of attention.

- I wanted him to romance me, watch movies in bed with me and give me endless kisses and cuddles.
- I wanted him to dress up for me and take me out to restaurants, family outings and go on holidays with the children when we could afford to.

In short, I wanted to feel like we were still dating for the rest of our lives together. I received absolutely everything I wanted in my marriage. The best part is, as soon as you start applying the twelve steps to your marriage, you will be on your way to becoming honeymooners forever.

Feel free to write to me, and let me know how you are going with the steps. I would love to hear from you.
phoebe@honeymoonersforever.com.au

May your love grow deeper daily.

With love,

Phoebe Hutchison.

* * *

Recommended Reading

8 Steps to a Remarkable Business.
Paul McCarthy

Ageless Body, Timeless Mind.
Deepak Copra, M.D.

Debt Buster.
Margaret Bertling

How to Get Rich.
Donald J. Trump

How to win friends and influence people.
Dale Carnegie

Fit for life.
Harvey and Marilyn Diamond

Life Strategies, Doing what works, Doing what matters.
Phillip C. McGraw, Ph.D.

Simple Abundance, A Daybook of Comfort and Joy.
Sarah Ban Breathnach

The Celestine Prophesy.
James Redfield

The Power is Within You.
Louise L. Hay

Toddler Taming, A parents guide to the first four years.
Dr Christopher Green

Vampires, Victims and Sex maniacs, A practical guide to overcoming limiting emotions and becoming all you dream to be.
Paul Barratt-Hassett

You Can Heal Your life.
Louise L. Hay

Your Sacred Self, Making the decision to be free.
Wayne W. Dwyer, M.D.